# BUILD A SUCCESSFUL RETIREMENT PLAN USING REAL ESTATE

A STEP-BY-STEP PATH TO EARLY RETIREMENT

MICHAEL STEVEN

www.TheBestSellerBooks.com

For more information:

Website: VAGPublishing.com

Email: Michael@TheBestSellerBooks.com

# CONTENTS

## REAL ESTATE INVESTMENT CHECKLIST

### (9 Calculators That Will Help You Achieve Success!)

This checklist includes:

❏ 9 important calculators that you should use to achieve success and head towards *Financial Freedom with Real Estate*

❏ Helpful links

❏ Plus receive future updates

Forget about yesterday and start thinking about tomorrow.

*"The past and the future are separated by a second, so make that second count!" ~ Quote from Carmine Pirone*

To receive your Free Real Estate Calculators Checklist, email me at:

michael@TheBestSellerBooks.com

*"The goal isn't more money. The goal is living life on your terms."*

— *CHRIS BROGAN*

# INTRODUCTION

Did you know that investing in real estate is an effective early retirement plan? In a study published by CNBC, nearly 40% of Americans are at risk of retiring near the poverty level. Now, if that isn't scary, I don't know what else is. What's even worse is that many people who are afraid of retiring broke tend to work harder so they can save for a comfortable retirement, and those whose savings did not meet up to their goal before their retirement age end up working even after retirement.

As someone who is aiming for an early retirement, your plan should not be about saving to reach that goal. What you should be looking into is how to get passive income so you can start an early retirement in record time. Saving for an early retirement is not a bad plan. However, it may not be the best plan because it will take longer for you to achieve that goal. Also, when you are retired, it will mean that your main source(s) of income will stop, and you will need something to fall back on. So, how can you have savings that will sustain you in retirement when you no longer have a major source of income? Think about that! Nevertheless, if you have passive income, there is no way you will be bothered about your survival during your retirement because passive income doesn't depend on whether you have a major source of income.

A self-made millionaire Sam Dogen, who retired at 34 in 2012, said investing in real estate was one of the major reasons he was able to retire at such an early age. I want to use this opportunity to show you how possible it is to have an early retirement with real estate investment.

Let's use Alan as a case study—Alan is a 40-year-old man with a **monthly income of $5,000,** and his **monthly expenses cost $4,000.** He has no debts or retirement savings, but he has saved **$25,000** to buy his own home. From Alan's profile, you can see that he needs $4,000 per month in passive income to retire early. So, we will be analyzing how Alan can go from $25,000 in savings to a comfortable early retirement in just five years through real estate investment.

## YEAR 1: HE INVESTS HIS SAVINGS AND BUYS DUPLEX #1

At the beginning of the year, Alan finds a local realtor who specializes in working with real estate investors. Together, they find an inexpensive little duplex in a low-cost-of-living section of town. Alan buys the duplex for $80,000, puts 20% down, and the remaining $9,000 is used to update the units and do some light repairs. After making the updates, the price of the duplex appreciates to $110,000. The property is now worth more than what Alan paid, so he can go back to his lender and arrange for a *cash-out* refinance. He can set up a new mortgage for 75% of the After Repair Value (ARV), allowing him to pull equity back out of the home.

Here's what that looks like in summary:

- Down payment: $16,000.
- Total mortgage: $64,000 ($540/month).
- Monthly mortgage payment (with tax & insurance): $540.
- Rehab: $9,000.
- Rent after rehab: $750/unit, or $1,500 total.
- ARV: $110,000.
- Total amount invested: $25,000.
- After six months of ownership, he refinances for 75% of ARV, $82,500 @5% interest.
- $18,500 cash out refinance.
- New mortgage payment with tax and insurance: $640/month.
- CapEx, vacancy, repairs, and property management: $450/month.
- Cash flow: $400/month (rounded for simplicity)

***End of year 1:***

- It took time to repair and rent each unit, so Alan's rental income for the year was $400/month for 10 months: $4,000
- His duplex appreciates at an average rate of 3% per year, therefore the value increases by $3,300.
- Total saved: $12,000 (regular monthly savings) + $4,000 (rental cash flow) + $18,500 (cash out refinance) = $34,500

## YEAR 2: ALAN BUYS DUPLEX #2

He now has more money saved, so he can invest in a better area of town. His realtor helps him buy a duplex for $100,000; he puts 20% down and uses the remaining amount for repairs ($14,000). He adds value to the duplex by adding a bedroom and bathroom to each unit, thereby increasing the rental income and overall home value. The ARV is $160,000.

- Down payment: $20,000.
- Total mortgage: $80,000 ($650/month).
- Monthly mortgage payment (with tax and insurance): $650.
- Rehab: $14,000.
- Rent after rehab: $1,000/unit or $2,000 total.
- ARV: $160,000.
- Total amount invested: $34,000.
- After six months of ownership, he refinances for 75% of ARV, $120,000 @5% interest.
- $40,000 cash out refinance.
- New mortgage payment with tax and insurance: $860/month.
- CapEx, vacancy, repairs, and property management: $550/month.
- Cash flow: $600/month

***End of year 2:***

- It took time to repair and rent each unit, so Alan's rental income for the year was $600/month for 10 months: $6,000.
- His duplex appreciates at an average rate of 3% per year, therefore the value increases by $4,800.
- Total saved: $12,000 (regular monthly savings) +

$6,000 (rental cash flow) + $40,000 (cash out refinance) = $58,000.
- Monthly cash flow: $1,000.

After 2 years, Alan is 25% closer to an early retirement.

## YEAR 3: ALAN DOES NOTHING BUT SAVE

- $12,000 from regular savings.
- $12,000 from rental income.
- Equity build: $3,500 from duplex #1 and $5,000 from duplex #2, or $8,500 total.
- Total annual savings: $24,000.
- Total overall savings: $82,000

## YEAR 4: ALAN BUYS FOURPLEX #1

After searching for a few months, Alan sees a fourplex in a nice area of town. It is in disrepair, so he contacts the owner. As it turns out, the owner would like to retire and would love to make an easy sale so he no longer has to manage the units. Alan arranges to purchase the fourplex for $375,000 with a 10% down payment. He agrees to owner financing at 7% interest with no early payoff penalty.

- Down payment: $37,500.
- Monthly mortgage payment: $2,250.
- Rehab: $40,000.
- Rent after rehab: $4,400.
- ARV: $440,000.
- Amount invested: $77,500.
- After six months of ownership, he refinances for $330,000 @6% interest.

- $110,000 cash out refinance.
- New mortgage payment with tax and insurance is $2000/month.
- CapEx, vacancy, repairs, and property management: $930/month.
- Cash flow: $1470/month.

Alan now owns two duplexes and a fourplex. His tenants pay the mortgage, taxes, and insurance for him and a property manager takes care of the daily management and filling of vacancies. Since he focused on properties that needed some repairs, he bought them below the market value, then added value with rehabilitation and refinanced them. This allowed him to pull money back out of each property in the form of equity. Coupled with a high savings rate, he was able to continue buying properties rather than becoming locked into just one investment property.

***End of year 4:***

Alan currently has:

- $4,500 in savings after purchasing and rehabbing the fourplex.
- $110,000 back from the refinance.
- Total of $114,500 ready to invest.
- Total monthly cash flow: $2,470.

Alan is now a little over halfway to early retirement! In the next year, he repeats the process and secures a similar fourplex. For simplicity, I'll keep the explanation the same.

## YEAR 5: BUY FOURPLEX #2

- Down payment: $37,500.
- Monthly mortgage payment: $2,250.
- Rehab: $40,000.
- Rent after rehab: $4,400.
- ARV: $440,000.
- Amount invested: $77,500.
- After six months of ownership, he refinances for $330,000 @6% interest.
- $110,000 cash out refinance.
- New mortgage payment with tax and insurance is $2000/month.
- CapEx, vacancy, repairs, and property management: $930/month.
- Cash flow: $1470/month.

***End of year 5:***

Alan's savings are now:

- $37,000 in savings after purchasing and rehabbing fourplex #2
- $110,000 back from the refinance.
- Total of $147,000 ready to invest.
- Cash flow: $3,940

Since Alan still has 25% equity in each property, and they appreciate an average of 3% per year, his net worth has improved significantly.

Alan's 5-year real estate investment portfolio in summary:

**Duplex #1:**

- Value at year 1: $113,300
- Value at year 2: $116,699
- Value at year 3: $120,200
- Value at year 4: $123,806
- Value at year 5: $127,520

**Duplex #2:**

- Value at year 2: $164,800
- Value at year 3: $169,744
- Value at year 4: $174,836
- Value at year 5: $180,081

**Fourplex #1:**

- Value at the end of year 4: $453,200
- Value at year 5: $466,800

**Fourplex #2:**

- Value at the end-of-year 5: $453,200

**Total property portfolio value: $1,227,600**
**Total equity: $307,000.**

In Alan's case, he started from a nest egg of $25,000, and it took him five full years to reach early retirement. However, if you start from $0, it will take a couple years of saving $1,000/month to build up the initial down payment and rehabilitation fund. Still, one of the many benefits to real estate investment is that through creative financing or private money loans, you can get a home for little or no money paid down. Another benefit is that you also don't have to wait a full year between investments. For these reasons, your path to early retirement could be even quicker than Alan's. Exciting right?

With so much information about real estate investment, I understand that you might be feeling overwhelmed, especially when you have little or no experience in this industry. Some questions that may be bugging your mind right now could be, *"How do I start investing in real estate? What path do I take? I'm not good at math, so how can I calculate numbers and do the financial projections? There are so many real estate investment options, which one do I choose? How many properties do I need to invest in for my retirement? When do I know it is okay to retire? Who do I ask to guide me in this journey?"*

I understand all these questions you have in mind and how overwhelming it can all be. I wouldn't be surprised if you are already thinking that this is becoming too complicated for you to handle and that you want to back down. But hey—I'm here to guide you. I wrote this book for you because I want to make it easier than it was for me when I started my journey in investing in real estate.

With over 30 years of experience in finance and investment, I have taught people how to get out and stay out of debt worth millions of dollars, buy and sell properties, and settle into an early retirement. As a mortgage director, I have invested over $1 billion in real estate, and helping you achieve financial freedom without a lot of money matters deeply to me because what I'm about to teach you in this book made me more money than I could have ever imagined. This is my way of giving back to society and helping people benefit from my success.

In this book, you will learn:

1. How to select the right investment property for you.
2. How to find the right financing for your investment property.
3. Computations for getting property at the right price.
4. How to find quality tenants.
5. How to negotiate with the seller.
6. Practical examples.
7. Contingency plans for unexpected events.
8. What to do when you reach your monthly rental income goal.
9. The essential people you will need to start your real estate investment journey.
10. How and when to add more rental properties.

If an early retirement is something you want, reading *Build a Successful Retirement Plan Using Real Estate* will benefit in teaching you:

- How you can **reduce your retirement number and retire earlier** by investing in rental properties.
- Alternative ways of financing your investment property that **don't require you to make a down payment.**
- Eight legal ways to **find real estate below market value** (and you won't need to cheat, lie, or make up numbers).
- The **#1 difference** in evaluating a property to live in versus a property to rent out.
- When you can realistically **make an offer below asking price** and still get it accepted by the seller.
- A **proven investment strategy** that will enable

you to add more rental properties consistently, even with limited funds.
- About **affordable renovations that add value to your property** and increase your rental rate, along with those that don't.

With all the amazing benefits you'll gain from reading this book, there is no doubt that it is the perfect guide for you. So, if you are ready to actualize your dream of an early retirement using real estate, why not get started reading ***Build a Successful Retirement Plan Using Real Estate*** immediately?

# CHAPTER ONE: PLAN YOUR RETIREMENT

In planning your retirement, there are a couple things you need to figure out or calculate. You need to know how much you will need to retire, which largely depends on the kind of lifestyle you want to live during retirement; calculate your retirement expenses (including travel and health); figure out your guaranteed source(s) of income and how much they bring in; and finally, decide how much you will need to save from your income to reach your early retirement goal.

Based on the kind of lifestyle you want to live during your retirement, you ought to have about 25 to 30 times your estimated annual expenses saved up or invested. Why I will always recommend investing over saving is because savings will definitely finish, since you will be spending out of it to sustain your lifestyle during retirement. Savings cannot produce passive income, and when you're always taking something out without any refill, it will eventually dry up. Investing, on the other hand, provides passive income and can give you peace of mind, knowing that you have money that can care for your needs.

## HOW TO PLAN YOUR RETIREMENT

**1. Define your own meaning of early retirement:** For some people, early retirement means not having to work or earn ever again; for others, it is not having to work again but still earning passive income. It could also mean leaving a 9-5 and establish a business or pick up a hobby that allows for flexible hours. There are different strokes for different folks. Thus, you have to define what early retirement means to you. This will be your first step in achieving your early retirement goal. If you don't define early retirement for yourself, you may not know how to get there.

**2. Track your income (from guaranteed sources) and expenses:** After defining what early retirement means to you, the next line of action is to figure out how to achieve it. The first step in discovering how to do so is to calculate, track, and keep records of your income and expenditure. Your income can include pension, social security from you and your spouse, monthly annuity payments, one-time sources like sale of a property, inheritance, or life insurance. Calculating the difference between your income and expenditure will give you insight into how much you can save for future investments or how to adjust your finances by increasing your income, cutting down on your expenses, or both.

**3. Know your numbers:** Say, for instance, you are 30 years old and plan to retire at 50. That means you will have 20 years to plan, save, and invest for your retirement. Let's assume you earn $6,000 monthly and your expenses total $4,000 per month. This means you will have $2,000 left. From this assumption, we can see that you need to earn at least $4,000 a month to live comfortably in retirement. So, if we further assume that you would live an extra 30 years—or 360 months—it means you should have a minimum of $1,440,000 saved. This is where it gets really interesting; if you were to save $2,000 every month to prepare for your retirement in 20 years (240 months) starting now, that would give you a total of $480,000, which will not cover your monthly living expenses for the extra 30 years you would be alive in retirement. When you fix your own numbers and do this calculation, you can see why I stated in my opening statement that investing is better than saving. Still using the numbers above, if you decide to save $2,000 every month for two years (24 months) consistently, at the end of those two years, you would have saved up $48,000, which is enough to invest into a rental property. When you get returns on your investment—when the 20 years are up and you want to retire—you will confidently have between 25 to 30 times your annual expenditure as investment. If the calculation seems daunting and you have some doubts because of potential recession or any other unforeseen circumstances, you can consult with a financial planner to help you draft an actionable plan.

*NB: When estimating your retirement expenses, it is important to include those your employer(s) currently pay for e.g. health insurance, also. The reason is that when you retire, such expenses will become your responsibility.*

**4. Spend less than you earn:** There are three categories of early retirement based on how people spend. These categories are: *FIRE, leanFIRE,* and *fatFIRE.* **FIRE** is an acronym for *Financial Independence Retire Early.* Anyone who falls under this category has their spending in line with the average US household expenditure, which is $60,000/year

($5,000/month). For those in the **leanFIRE** category, they spend less than the average American and live on a lean budget. It also includes those who have saved up to 25 times their annual expenses. Finally, people in the **fatFIRE** category are those who spend more than they earn. If there is any category anyone should strive to be in, it is the leanFIRE category. Inasmuch as being in this category is profitable, it is better to invest than save. Finally, if you want to improve your savings or move from either the FIRE or fatFIRE categories to the leanFIRE category, cut down on your rent (if you need to get a cheaper apartment, do so), transportation, shopping, and eating out. These are some ways you can save on costs and improve your savings. But do not forget that the essence of saving is so you can have enough to invest with.

**5. Take advantage of your income:** Saving is not the most effective retirement plan. Although I cannot dispute how having savings is good, I do not agree that you should allow your savings to sit in one place. Instead of piling up your savings, get it to work for you by investing in lucrative side hustles, such as real estate investment. The good thing about having passive income is that they can generate enough to cover your monthly expenses, which in turn will leave you with more room to save money for future investments.

**6. Consider using an employer-retirement account and IRAs:** An IRA is a type of account set up in a financial institution for the purpose of saving for retirement with a tax-free growth or on a tax-deferred basis. There are three types of IRA: *Traditional IRA, Rollover IRA,* and *Roth IRA.* Employer-sponsored retirement plans and IRAs are beneficial regarding tax advantages and investment growth. If, for instance, you can contribute up to $19,000 pretax to a

401(k) and $6,000 to a traditional IRA, you can get a tax deduction on your current year's tax return. However, the downside to stacking your retirement accounts when planning for an early retirement is the restrictions on withdrawals. You will be unable to withdraw any money from your 401(k) without penalty until you've reached the age of 59 and a half. However, you can withdraw contributions (excluding earnings) from your Roth IRA, tax-free, at any time.

7. **Consider paying off your mortgage before retirement:** When you are preparing for an early retirement, removing consumer debt with high interest rates is your best bet. However, paying off a mortgage early with good terms isn't so straightforward; for some, the peace of mind of being liability-free is worth it, whereas others may argue the money saved in interest payments pale in comparison to potential investment returns. I'll give an example—a retiree named Tommy retired nearly 10 years ago at 51, after a more than a three-decade career in telecom. He never earned a six-figure salary but focused on saving consistently since his 20s and living frugally with his wife and three kids. In one of his blog posts, he said his biggest regret was not paying off his mortgage before retirement.

8. **Create best-case and worst-case scenarios:** Best-case scenarios include above-average returns, average life expectancy, and low inflation, whereas worst-case scenarios may include below-average returns, above-average life expectancy, and high inflation. Nevertheless, your retirement estimates should still be able to cover your expenses in the worst-case scenario. Also, incorporate inflation in your projections or calculate the present value of the amount you need on your retirement date.

Now that you have seen how to plan your early retirement, it is important to know the advantages of investing in real estate rental properties, rather than saving for early retirement.

## ADVANTAGES OF INVESTING IN RENTAL PROPERTIES FOR EARLY RETIREMENT

1. Steady income.
2. Long-term financial security.
3. Tax benefits.
4. Covering mortgage payments.
5. Real estate appreciation.
6. Inflation.
7. You are your own boss.

The amount of cash flow rental properties bring in as passive income depends on how much you spend to maintain the property. In simpler terms, if the projection of a rental property is that it will bring in a revenue of $1,500 monthly, and your expenses on that property per month is $800, it means the passive income from that property is $700 monthly. With this knowledge, you can determine if the passive income from the rental property will help you reach early retirement in record time, using your monthly expenses in retirement as the yardstick.

Rental income also grows along with inflation. Essentially, you create your own inflation-adjusted pension using real estate income properties. For example, although the average inflation rate for the past 100 years has been 3 percent, an average rate of 3.9 percent occurred between the closure of World War II and 2013. Likewise, the average rate of inflation exceeded 6 percent between 1981 and 1994.

In conclusion, you will need less money saved to retire

early when you have consistent cash flows from your rental properties and can meet your income needs with a smaller net worth. Also, with regular rental income coming in, even beyond retirement, you will need to access less money from your savings and investments, which then means you can have a lot more saved than if you were to rely mainly on your savings and investments during retirement.

## NUMBERS TEMPLATE FOR EARLY RETIREMENT PLAN

I will show you examples using two different scenarios of how hard-working investors could retire within 10 to 25 years, depending on their savings rates, income, and self-discipline with investing.

1. A 35-year-old who wants to retire in 25 years by age 60.
2. A 35-year-old who wants to retire in 10 years by age 45.

## EXAMPLE 1: 35-YEAR-OLD RETIRING IN 25 YEARS (AGE 60)

Rachael and Justin are both 35 years old, and they bought a $200,000 home five years ago with a 5% down, 30-year, $907/month, and a 4% fixed-interest loan. They also recently paid off the last of their personal debt (cars, student loans, etc.). So, they're now ready to begin building wealth in earnest through both their 401k and real estate investments. In the beginning, their assets looked like this:

- $28,000 = current equity in their house.
- $25,000 = 401k balances.
- $25,000 = cash saved for real estate investing.

Going forward, their savings and investment assumptions looked like this:

- $150,000 = collective earnings per year
- $30,000 = investment savings per year
- 8.175% = average return on investments over time (401k and real estate)
- 25 years = target date for retirement
- $150,000 = target retirement withdrawal income

Their wealth-building plan will have three parallel paths.

1. Contribute $10,000 per year to their 401k, receive an employer match, and invest in broadly diversified index funds with the lowest expense ratios possible.
2. Use $20,000 per year to buy a small portfolio of rental properties that will be owned free and clear of debt well before their retirement date, using the rental debt snowball method. A portion of the rental income will also be saved for extra cash reserves.
3. Make the minimum payment on their home mortgage until it's completely paid off in 25 years. This will eliminate the need for housing mortgage or rent payments when they retire.

After 25 years, Rachael and Justin have had a total net worth of over $3,100,000. The breakdown between the different categories looks like this:

| | Original Value | Growth Rate | Future Value |
|---|---|---|---|
| Principle Residence (House) | $200,000 | 2.81% | $400,000 |
| Cash | $25,000 | n/a | $100,000 |
| Stocks/Bonds in 401k | $25,000 | 8.175% | $928,000 |
| Rental Properties | $25,000 | 8.175% | $1,678,000 |
| TOTAL NET WORTH: | $275,000 | | $3,106,000 |

And their income looks like:

| | Future Value | Withdrawal Rate | Future Income |
|---|---|---|---|
| Principle Residence (House) | $400,000 | 0% | $0 |
| Cash | $100,000 | 1% | $1,000 |
| Stocks/Bonds in 401k | $928,000 | 4% | $37,120 |
| Rental Properties | $1,678,000 | 7% | $117,460 |
| TOTAL INCOME: | $3,106,000 | 5% | $155,580 |

In this, I assumed their rental properties produced net rental income at a rate of 7%. I also assumed they could withdraw 4% of their 401k portfolio each year without penalty, now that they're over the IRS threshold age of 59.5. And finally, I assumed their cash reserves received 1% yield per year. Although these results are in future dollars (i.e. worth less because of the value erosion of inflation), you can see that Rachael and Justin met their goal of $150,000 per year. Their $2,706,000 of investments ($928,000 in the 401k, $1,678,000 in real estate, and $100,000 in cash) now support them financially. They also have no housing payment to worry about now that the mortgage is paid off.

It is noteworthy that if the $2,706,000 had only been in traditional investments, a 4% withdrawal rate would reduce their spendable withdrawals from $155,000 to $108,000. Because of this, they might have had to keep working longer to garner a larger net worth, or they might have had to settle for a lower withdrawal amount. However, their real estate investments and the higher income they produced allowed them to avoid that choice.

## EXAMPLE 2: EARLY RETIREMENT IN 10 YEARS

Kim and Steve are both 35 years old and applied the strategy of house hacking (when you buy a small multi-unit real estate property, live in one unit, and rent out the others) to buy a house worth $200,000 with a rentable garage apartment. Their house financing terms were the same with a 5% down, 30-year, $907/month, 4% fixed-interest loan. But by renting the garage apartment on Airbnb, they easily earn $1,000/month or more, eliminating their entire mortgage payment. Also, they save $82,000 per year.

At the start, their assets looked like this:

- $28,000 = current equity in their house.
- $25,000 = 401k balances.
- $25,000 = cash saved for real estate investing.

And going forward, their savings and investment assumptions looked like this:

- $150,000 = collective earnings per year.
- $82,000 = extra savings for investing per year.
- 8.175% = average return on investments over time (401k and real estate).
- 10 years = target date for early retirement.
- $60,000 = minimum early retirement withdrawal income.

Their wealth-building plan will also have three parallel paths.

1. Contribute $20,000 per year to their 401k, receive an employer match, and invest in broadly diversified index funds with the lowest expense ratios possible.
2. Use $62,000 per year to buy a small portfolio of rental properties and pay off the mortgages aggressively using the rental debt snowball method.
3. Make the minimum payment on their home mortgage for 25 years. Of course, they'll still owe money on the debt at their target early retirement date in 10 years. However, their house hacking plan using Airbnb effectively eliminates their out of pocket housing expense.

After 10 years at the age of 45, Kim and Steve have a total net worth of $1,456,900. The breakdown between different categories looks like this:

| | Original Value | Growth Rate | Future Value |
|---|---|---|---|
| House Value | $200,000 | 1% | $222,000 |
| Debt Balance | $172,000 | | $122,600 |
| Principle Residence Equity | $28,000 | 14% | $99,400 |
| Cash | $25,000 | n/a | $50,000 |
| Stocks/Bonds in 401k | $25,000 | 8.175% | $347,000 |
| Rental Properties | $25,000 | 8.175% | $960,500 |
| TOTAL NET WORTH: | $103,000 | | $1,456,900 |

And their income looks like:

| | Future Value | Withdrawal Rate | Future Income |
|---|---|---|---|
| Principle Residence (House) | $99,400 | 0% | $0 |
| Cash | $50,000 | 1% | $500 |
| Stocks/Bonds in 401k | $347,000 | 0% | $0 |
| Rental Properties | $960,500 | 7% | $67,235 |
| TOTAL INCOME: | $1,456,900 | 5% | $67,735 |

Like example 1, I assumed their rental properties produced net rental income at a rate of 7% and their cash produced 1% interest. Because they are too young to withdraw from a 401k penalty free, they would withdraw 0% from retirement accounts. So, they have no choice than to let it continue to grow and compound. Even if no more contributions are made, at their current growth rate of 8.175%, the $347,000 could grow to around $1,128,000 by the time they are 60 years old.

Kim and Steve now have the luxury of covering all their living expenses ($60,000/year) with rental income. True to the hold fast phase described above, their net worth will stay intact until they can reach retirement age and access a retirement account and social security funds. But because they are only living off rental income and they keep their expenses at a reasonable level, their net worth will likely continue to grow at a good rate, even after early retirement. They'll continue to build equity in their home, their untouched holdings in their 401k account will continue to grow, and the value of their real estate investments will likely grow at the rate of inflation.

So, you have now seen two examples related to aspiring retirees in their 30s. But these examples are different from those beginning this journey later in life. If someone is behind on retirement savings or digging themselves out of prior financial challenges, they may need a different approach.

## CHAPTER SUMMARY

- Based on the kind of lifestyle you want to live during your retirement, you ought to have about 25 to 30 times your estimated annual expenses saved up or invested.
- Saving is not the most effective retirement plan. Although it is still great and even important to have a savings account, I do not agree that you should allow your savings to sit in one place. Instead of piling up your savings, get it to work for you by investing in lucrative side hustles, such as real estate investment.
- In conclusion, you require less money saved to retire early when you have consistent cash flows from your rental properties and can meet your income needs with a smaller net worth.

In the next chapter, you will learn more about investing in rental properties.

# CHAPTER TWO: MORE ABOUT INVESTING IN RENTAL PROPERTIES

Now that you know the total rental income you are aiming for, you can start building your rental property portfolio, one property at a time. Most likely, you will be unable to cover your entire monthly retirement income requirement with just one rental property.

Rental properties provide long-term cash flow that does not eat up your principal investment. With a significant amount of cash flow, you can generate a mostly passive income that will last as long as you own rental properties. Your tenants' rent will pay all your expenses for you, including the mortgage, and leave extra money left over for you. Also, rents will eventually go up with inflation, just like the stock market always goes up, but your mortgage payment will stay the same. Given enough time, your tenants will pay off your mortgage, and your cash flow will really increase.

In real estate investing, the *buy and hold strategy* is one of the most popular forms of investment. The ***buy and hold strategy*** is when an investor buys a property to own over a long period (five to 30 years). The value of that property increases over time, and the investor enjoys a stable cash flow from the rental income of that property.

Long-term ownership in the buy and hold strategy does not mean the property has to be leased long term. The owner (investor) can lease only during the summer or for short term corporate rental that yields higher returns. The buy and hold rental investment is a simple way to earn passive income, especially when looking at an early retirement.

Apart from how the buy and hold strategy is common and easy to invest in, below are some other reasons it is preferable to other real estate investment strategies like *fix and flip, value-add, REIT, and wholesaling.*

1. **Predictable and ongoing passive income:** Before buying a property, you can calculate how much money you will make from it monthly. You can do this calculation by using a rental property ROI calculator or analyzing the real estate cash flow. If you have a long-term tenant, it means you are looking at having long-term passive income, regardless of the repairs you might have to take care of. You will also have the option of contracting the repairs of your rental property to a property management company.

2. **Tax advantages:** The IRS allows investors to take tax deductions for any legitimate expense they run into while managing their rental property. For example, as an investor, you can deduct your mortgage interest payments, maintenance costs, insurance premiums (including rent default insurance), property taxes, tenant screening fees (if you pay them rather than charging them directly to the applicants), property management fees, some closing costs, and legal costs, such as lease agreements. You can even deduct for paper expenses like depreciation! Here comes the most interesting part: when you eventually go to sell, you'll

pay the lower capital gains tax rate—instead of your regular income tax rate—because you held the property as a long-term investment.

**3. Hedge against inflation:** Similar to natural disasters, inflation can happen, and there's hardly anything you can do to stop it. However, unlike natural disasters that affect real estate negatively, inflation is actually an advantage to a buy and hold real estate investment. Instead of an investor having to worry about inflation eating at their returns, rent rises with inflation, or in some cases, even faster than it. This means that as long as there's inflation, your returns will keep rising.

**4. Value appreciation:** One outstanding benefit of the buy and hold real estate investment strategy is the appreciation of such properties. As long as the property you bought is in a highly sought-after residential area, then the value will continue to appreciate.

Everything with advantages will also have disadvantages. After learning about the advantages of the buy-and-hold strategy for rental properties, it is important that you also know some disadvantages associated with this strategy, so you can make informed decisions.

**1. Failure of tenants to pay rent:** When tenants fail to pay rent, the owner of the property will have no choice but to evict them and look for new ones that will pay. I mean, it is business and nothing personal. However, property owners stand the risk of erring tenants, leaving their property with some damages that will cost the owner to have to fix before they can put it up for lease again. One way to avoid this happening to you is by screening the applicants carefully.

Other solutions include buying rent default insurance and keeping emergency funds for repairs and insurance deductibles.

**2. Damage to property:** As stated earlier, some tenants can damage your property at the time of their evacuation, and you really won't be able to stop them from leaving. You can avoid this outcome by carrying out proper screening—call their previous tenants and find out if they vacated their property in good shape. You might also want to collect a high security deposit that will be enough to cover the cost of large repairs if the need arises. When it's time to vacate and everything is in order, you must refund this fee. This is also another screening technique; responsible tenants will not object to this, since they know they will not have to worry and will leave your property in good shape.

**3. Vacancies:** Investors stand the risk of having an unoccupied property for some time. The best way to prevent this is by investing in a highly sought-after residential area. You can also include a vacancy rate when you predict your cash flow with a rental property ROI calculator. Finally, make sure you set some money aside for your mortgage every month so you can afford to pay, even when you have no tenants.

4. It takes much time, experience, and education to figure out the best markets to invest in and where you can make money.

5. In most cases, you will need a large amount of money to invest, including reserves.

6. It takes time to manage properties, or you will have to pay 8-10% of the monthly rent to a property manager.

Now that you have seen both the benefits and disadvantages of using the buy and hold strategy for investing in rental properties, it is time to learn *how* to invest in rental properties, starting from the basics of investing.

## BASICS OF INVESTING IN RENTAL PROPERTIES

1. Buy rental properties below market value.
2. Buy rental properties that create cash flow.
3. Do not count on appreciation unless you have a solid plan in place to deal with market down turns.
4. Find a great lender that will help you leverage your money.
5. Have a great team in place that can help you buy rental properties: real estate agent, lender, contractor, and attorney if needed.
6. Stay on top of your tenants and maintenance.
7. Have an emergency fund set up for unexpected costs.

## BUY RENTAL PROPERTIES BELOW MARKET VALUE

When you research the market you want to invest in and buy properties below the market value, it will save you from having to deal with certain potential problems that could come with the investment. The main benefit of buying properties below market value is that you can sell them without any loss if that property has no cash flow, and you can decide to exit the investment.

The truth is, it is not easy to buy real estate below market value; however, it is not impossible. If you want to buy real estate below market value, you will need a real estate agent who can act fast because deals do not last long. Some places where you can get great sales include *estate sales, REOs, short sales, auctions, traditional sales,* and *off market.*

Often, a property will be underpriced because it requires repairs. So, if you're going to buy such property, make sure the total cost of repairs and the property is still below the market value.

## BUY RENTAL PROPERTIES THAT CASH FLOW

Cash flow is defined as the net amount you make from your rental property every month. For example, if you charge $2,500 for rent and pay $1,000 for expenses, your monthly cash flow from this rental property is $1,500. One amazing thing about buying properties with good cash flow is that the money will keep flowing every month, as long as you own the property and inflation helps increase the price of rent too, and as stated earlier, your tenants will pay the mortgage and you'll still have leftover money.

Buying just one rental property won't help you retire early—you will need multiple properties that provide cash flow every month to care for your needs during retirement. When calculating cash flow, many investors do not include maintenance and vacancy expenses. For me, I like to assume I will use between 10% and 25% of the monthly rent as maintenance expenses, depending on how old and in what condition my property is in. Some other costs to consider with cash flow include HOA fees, utilities (if you'll be paying them), and management fees if you use a property manager.

Many people cannot afford to buy rental properties in one go, so let's assume you will get a loan. For this reason, you will need rental properties that will create a decent amount of cash flow so you can pay off the debt you owe.

## MUST-HAVE TEAM OF PROFESSIONALS FOR REAL ESTATE INVESTORS

As I stated earlier, if you want to buy real estate property at a price lower than the market value, you need a real estate agent. Furthermore, real estate agents are not the only people you need to make your purchase and property maintenance seamless. You will need additional professionals before and after the purchase is done. You must also make sure they are good at their jobs, have tangible work experience, and have proof of competence.

1. **Real estate agent:** A real estate agent is one of the most important team members that an investor will need. A real estate agent with a lot of investment experience in your local market can help you decide how much you should offer for a property, and they can even point out things that aren't in the listing. In addition, your real estate agent can bring you off-market deals they hear about and save you time in the negotiating and purchasing processes. Finally, your real estate agent can help you find or recommend any of the other professionals on this list.

2. **Property manager:** Hiring a property manager may seem unrealistic to you because there's likely no one who will love and manage your property better than you can. I totally understand your point of view, but here's why I would still recommend you get a property manager—although you may have the time to run around and fix faulty appliances in your rental properties or handle emergency evictions or a tenant's call at odd hours, have you considered that paying someone as little as 8-10% of your rental income monthly may be

worth the lowered stress levels? Think about all the good that having someone who can take care of your property can do for your general wellbeing.

**3. Mortgage professional:** Many investors have a mortgage broker who does the groundwork of scouting for investment property loans on their behalf, while others have a go-to contact for a specific lender. Whichever path you choose, you should have someone whom you trust to help you through the loan process, if the need arises.

**4. Real estate attorney:** It is never a bad idea to have someone who knows the law on your side, just in case things go awry. This is especially true in the case of a sudden eviction or if a tenant sues you; it is good to have an attorney who is experienced in real estate matters. Your real estate agent should be able to recommend a good attorney to you.

**5. Insurance agent:** Most property or casualty insurers can write insurance policies on investment properties; however, you will want one with experience in working with investors and their lenders (if any). For instance, many asset-based lenders have specific and bizarre insurance requirements, so you'll want an insurer who can deal with your mortgage servicer. Your current homeowners insurance agent is a good place to start—that is, if you're satisfied with their service, but it's important to ask about their investor-specific experience.

**6. Home inspector:** You won't always have all your *t*'s crossed and *i*'s dotted when it comes to inspecting a home, so you *will* need a home inspector. Now, a property may look like it is in perfect condition, but there may be areas that need repairs that the home inspector will bring to your notice. With their first-hand knowledge, you will be able to make an informed decision as to whether you should pay for the repairs or pass on the property.

7. **Appraiser:** It is okay to carry out your own research when figuring out how much a property is worth. However, when you hire an appraiser, they can then give you an accurate assessment of how much the property is worth. Many investors think that hiring an appraiser is a waste of money, but the fact is that many investors tend to overestimate a property. An appraiser will give the honest truth about how much a property is really worth, especially if it is vacant.

8. **Accountant:** Inasmuch as real estate has an amazing tax advantage, calculating rental taxes can be challenging, especially when you own several properties. For example, do you know how to calculate depreciation accurately or report it to the IRS? Did you also know that your mortgage interest on rental properties is deducted differently compared to the interest on your personal residence mortgage? Hiring a Certified Public Accountant (CPA) will help you keep your rental income and expenses in order and calculate your deductions accurately.

9. **Contractor/handyman:** No matter how rent-ready your property is, something is bound to get faulty sooner or later, and this is where you will need a handyman or contractor. They must be able to come to your aid in record time while also charging reasonable fees. They must also be efficient at their jobs and able to provide lasting solutions through their fixes. If you don't know where to find reliable contractors, you can ask your property manager or real estate manager to link you up with whom they use.

As a real estate investor, the list of people above will either make or break you. You could get an amazing property, but if you don't have someone to market it for you, it will sit vacant for weeks, which conversely means that you will be losing money. If you have faulty appliances that require immediate fixing, and there's no reliable person to fix things around , there's only so much discomfort your tenants will bear before they move out. So choose your team carefully.

## PROPERTIES THAT MAKE THE BEST RENTALS

Having seen the basics and how to invest in real estate using rental properties, it is important you know what kind of rental properties to invest in. The type of rental property you go for will depend on your investment strategy and objectives. However, generally, some things you should consider when choosing the type of rental property to invest in include *the best cities/towns, rent laws, home prices, proximity to retail and transit, quality of the neighborhood, tax districts, current rental housing market,and your finances, risk tolerance, and property management skills.*

1. Single-family rental houses.
2. Multi-family apartments/condos.
3. Small multi-family properties e.g. duplexes, triplexes, fourplexes.
4. Student housing.
5. High rise and low rise apartments.

Investors like to invest in the properties listed above because of cash flow. I'll also show you the benefits and pitfalls of each of these rental property choices.

## SINGLE-FAMILY RENTAL HOUSES

Single-family homes are normally bought for price appreciation because their price-to-rent ratio is high. With this type of property, you will be managing one tenant per time. Single-family houses are a more liquid investment than multi-family homes, and they are easier to sell. However, there is a higher risk in owning one property with a smaller pool of potential renters because of the higher rental price. Furthermore, if you are in California, it will be more difficult to create ROI from an expensive home; however, in up-and-coming cities such as Philadelphia, Omaha, or Charlotte, the price may be just right.

## MULTI-FAMILY APARTMENTS/CONDOS

As the owner of several apartments in the same building, it may help you to buy more properties and enjoy cheaper management costs, since it can give you more cash flow and you can buy two apartments for the price of one house. Also, because the demand for apartments is high, you can still get a good rental price on an apartment, even in a B-grade building. But unfortunately, the *Homeowners Association (HOA)* fees for owning this type of property isn't cheap. Another major disadvantage with owning a multi-family house is that it will involve more tenants, meaning more issues or problems that you may have to face.

## SMALL MULTI-FAMILY PROPERTIES

These cost less per unit than single-family, rent for about the same, and help save a lot on maintenance by making you replace just one roof rather than four different ones. As an investor, do not settle for any property with fewer than $200 dollars per door in cash flow per month after mortgage and expenses are paid.

## STUDENT HOUSING

Like other forms of housing, student housing is in big demand and will likely continue to be because some colleges and universities are no longer providing accommodations; these units can allow more beds per unit, thus maximizing your rental income.

## HIGH RISE AND LOW RISE APARTMENTS

**High rise** apartments are generally the most affordable type of apartment or condo out there. They are often located near CBDs, transit, and employment, and they appeal to millennials whose salaries are quickly rising. Tenants with kids or who do not like heights usually go for **low rise** apartments, as they are easier to maintain and renovate than condos 25 to 60 floors at the top of a tall building. The more units you have, the lower the per unit cost that property management companies will charge, and the better the financing you might get from banks.

Now that you have learned about some of the rental properties that you can invest in, it is time to look at the things you must recognize in prospective rental properties before investing in them.

## THINGS TO CONSIDER BEFORE BUYING A RENTAL PROPERTY

Knowing how to evaluate a rental property and recognize if it is a good investment and fit for you is a vital skill that every real estate investor must have. If you cannot do this, then there is absolutely no way you can be successful as a real estate investor. Below are nine things you should look out for when buying a rental property.

**1. Profitable rental market:** There is no point in purchasing a rental property if you won't be making any money from it. Generally speaking, I follow the rule of thumb that says that the monthly rent of a property should at least be 1% of its purchase price. So, say for instance that I purchase a single-family property for $100,000. I should be able to rent it out at $1,000 monthly. However, the price for the monthly rent will still depend on the interest rate, down payment of the property, purchase price, and variable costs of taxes and insurance. I'll use another example to explain this. Let's assume I purchased a $150,000 property and put down 20%, for a total mortgage amount of $120,000. At 5% Annual Percentage Rate (APR), the monthly mortgage payment for a 30-year loan would be around $644, including principal and interest but before insurance and taxes. For a 15-year loan, which is what I would choose, I would owe $949 per month in principal and interest. Now, assuming my property taxes were around $250 per month and my landlord's insurance policy was around $100 per month, my total housing payment would be approximately $1,200. If most single-family homes in the area I bought the rental property rent for well over $1,500 per month, this means I could turn a $300 profit and pay off my home in 15 years or less. With this explanation, you should be able to see why buying properties in profitable locations is the key to investment success.

**2. Simple landscaping:** Sometimes, less is actually more. The fact that you like mowing your lawn and grooming flowers doesn't mean other people will like it. So, as much as it is in your power, buy rental properties with simple landscaping that will not require too much effort from your tenants to care for.

**3. The number of bedrooms:** Now this will depend largely on the area the rental property is located in. If it is in a family-oriented area, it will only make sense that you find properties that can accommodate families. If the property is located in a student area, then you obviously cannot be looking for properties that can accommodate families in such an area.

**4. Major updates completed:** When buying a property, it is near impossible to find one that will please you 100%. You could look at the floors and absolutely hate it, and that's fine. But you should remember that you are not the one who would be staying in the apartment, and as long as the floors are functional, there is no *ugliness* that a little interior designing cannot fix. It is also okay to buy a rental property that needs minor fixes or renovation; however, the major ones such as roofing and HVAC systems should be functional and in good shape.

**5. Appealing neighborhood:** As explained in point three, this will also depend largely on the area that the property is located in. But the bottom line is that the more convenient a rental property is—which is relative to the surroundings and individual preferences—the more people will find it appealing.

**6. Low property taxes.**

7. **Properties with noticeable upkeep:** When you see the outward appearance of a property, you can easily tell whether

or not that property was cared for. Buying a rental property that was poorly cared for will definitely mean more repair expenses for you, which is something you should try to minimize as much as you can. Beyond the outward appearance, there are some more subtle areas you should check to know if they were properly cared for or not. An example is the HVAC system, and you should check that it hasn't been damaged in any way.

**8. Brick or low-maintenance exterior:** Fixing up the exterior of a building is expensive when calculating the cost. So go for properties with a brick or low-maintenance exterior.

**9. No water issues:** Check the plumbing, making sure there are no rings of water droplets in the ceiling, pools of water after it rains, or leakages anywhere.

Apart from the nine points above, there are other tried and trusted tools and metrics that can help you evaluate a rental property you are interested in buying.

- Use a rental property calculator.
- Calculate the Net Operating Income (NOI), which is the ***rental property income – operating expenses.*** The result must be positive; otherwise, don't invest in it.
- Capitalization rate (Cap Rate), which is the ***(NOI/Purchase price) X 100.***
- Cash on Cash Return (CoC), which is calculated as ***Annual cash flow (including mortgage payments)/Total cash invested X100.***

If this seems too complex for you to calculate or understand, it may be indicating that you need an accountant in your real estate investment team.

## WHAT TO AVOID WHEN BUYING A RENTAL PROPERTY

- **Septic systems:** Opt for a town sewer.
- **Homes built before 1996:** You will need to check for lead, asbestos, proper wiring, UFFI, polybutylene water pipes, etc.
- **Buying one unit inside a duplex or triplex:** It is better to buy the whole thing.
- **Rent-controlled areas.**

At this point in this chapter, and with all the knowledge you have about rental properties, it is now time to analyze the number of rental properties you will need to invest in so you can reach your early retirement goal.

## HOW MANY RENTAL PROPERTIES DO I NEED TO INVEST IN?

Now that you have seen how to start investing in real estate with rental properties, the kind of rental properties to invest in, how to set up a team for your real estate investment, and what to look out for when buying a rental property, let's do some calculations to see how many rental properties you will need to invest in for an early retirement.

There are retirement calculators that can help you with the calculations you need; however, for rental income, it will be better and even easier to do the math yourself and manually. I will show you five easy steps you can use to calculate the number of properties you will need for an early retirement. Let's get started.

Real estate retirement math has three variables, namely:

1. Your expenses in retirement **(E).**
2. Your wealth invested in real estate **(W).**
3. The conservative income yield, or cash-on-cash return on that wealth **(r).**

*The basic formula is this:* ***W x r** = **E** or **E** ÷ **r** = **W***

Let's go back to Alan from the introduction as our example. Remember that Alan's expenses in retirement will be $48,000 per year ($4,000 monthly). Let us then assume that he can find properties with a 10% cash-on-cash return. This means that he needs to invest a wealth (equity) of $480,000 into rental properties.

**E ÷ r = W**
**$48,000 ÷ 10% = W**
**$480,000 = W**

If Alan's math doesn't work for your situation, you can change each of these three variables as needed. For example, if your expenses will be $100,000 per year, you may need to invest $1 million instead of $480,000

**$100,000 ÷ 10% = W**
**$1,000,000 = W**

So, the math begins with your retirement expenses **(E),** and you will have to decide what that number is. Then you fix in **(r),** your cash-on-cash return assumption (e.g. 10%), which is the cash yield you can expect from your rental properties. The answer you will get is the amount of wealth **(W)** you need to either invest (if you already have the capital) or save. This math is easy to do, right? However, doing this math in real life situations is a little trickier, so I will show you how with the example below.

| Rental Property Assumptions | |
|---|---|
| Property Type: | Single Family Houses |
| Market Location: | • "Middle America" (i.e. south, midwest, and other parts of the U.S. where rent to value ratios are reasonable)<br>• a medium-sized city with a growing population and good long-term economic prospects<br>• a median-priced neighborhood (not the lowest, not the highest) |
| Total Cost of Each Property (Purchase, Closing Costs, Repairs) | $120,000 |
| Cash Investment Per Property | $30,000 |
| Mortgage Details | $90,000 principal (4.4% interest, 30 years, $450/month principal & interest payment) |
| Total Rental Income | $1,200 / month |
| Operating Expenses | -$500 / month |
| Net Operating Income | $700 / month |

In a perfect world, each house would be built for low-maintenance renting with a large crawl space, masonry or brick exterior siding, and hardwood and tile floors inside for inexpensive tenant turnovers, and have wonderful neighbors/tenants. But since the world is not perfect, getting all of that may be you wanting to have your cake and eat it too.

Since we are looking at real life situations, I will use two different rental properties for the calculations. The goal in both examples will be $84,000 per year in rental income (pre-tax).

1. The leveraged rental retirement portfolio.
2. The free and clear retirement portfolio.

## THE LEVERAGED RENTAL RETIREMENT PORTFOLIO

This type of rental retirement portfolio involves debt leverage.

1. 28 rental properties.
2. Total cost = $3,360,000 ($120,000 per property).
3. $840,000 equity capital invested ($30,000 per property).
4. $2,520,000 debt financing ($90,000 per property).
5. Total rental income/month = $33,600 ($1,200 per property).
6. Operating Expenses/month = -$14,000 (-$500 per property).
7. Net operating income/month = $19,600 ($700 per property)
8. Mortgage payments/month = -$12,600 (-$450 per property).
9. Total net positive cash flow/month = $7,000 ($250 per property).
10. Total net positive cash flow/year = $84,000.

Using the retirement formula above, we can calculate our cash-on-cash yield as follows:

**$840,000 x r = $84,000**
**r = 10%**

There are advantages and disadvantages to this investment portfolio.

***Advantages:***

1. You lock in low-interest, long-term debt secured

by quality rental properties. This is a GREAT inflation hedge.

2. In addition to cash flow, you will also receive growth from amortization of loans ($41,356 in just your first year of the loans).
3. You have the potential for price and rent appreciation, since you bought these in a solid location, which could send your returns off the chart in the future.

***Disadvantages:***

1. There are 28 properties to care for as an asset and/or property manager. Without strong systems, this could be a hassle.
2. Financing for 28 properties at those attractive terms could be challenging (probably the weakest link of this portfolio).
3. The next Great Depression could expose the entire portfolio to a risk of loss. Would you have cash reserves to survive on if rent craters by 25% or even 50%? Few investors could survive that, which is something to think about, even if the chances are very small.

## THE FREE AND CLEAR RETIREMENT PORTFOLIO

This type of rental retirement portfolio does not involve debt.

1. 10 rental properties.

2. Total cost = $1,200,000 ($120,000 per property).

- $1,200,000 equity capital invested ($120,000 per property).
- $0 debt financing.

3. Total rental income/month = $12,000 ($1,200 per property).

- Operating expenses/month = -$5,000 (-$500 per property).
- Net operating income/month = $7,000 ($700 per property).
- Mortgage payments/month = $0.

4. Total net positive cash flow/month = $7,000 ($700 per property).

- Total net positive cash flow/year = $84,000.

Thus, we can calculate our cash on cash yield as follows:

**$1,200,000 x r = $84,000**
**r** = 7%

***Advantages:***

1. Asset and property management is relatively simple. I could manage this number and type of properties part-time easily while traveling and enjoying life. A third-party property manager could make it even more passive.
2. Low deflation risk. Even during the next Great Depression, rent could be lowered or even bartered for goods and services, if needed.

3. Benefit from price and rent appreciation if and when that comes.

***Disadvantages:***

1. Higher equity capital requirement ($1,200,000) means it could take longer to reach your retirement goal.
2. Less attractive inflation hedge compared to having a leveraged portfolio (although growth is less of a concern in a mature portfolio, as long as it generally keeps up with inflation).

## FIVE STEPS TO HELP YOU CALCULATE THE NUMBER OF RENTAL PROPERTIES YOU WILL NEED TO INVEST IN FOR AN EARLY RETIREMENT

**1. Know your current personal expenses:** The first practical step to planning for an early retirement is to know your expenses. Once you can put a figure to how much you spend per annum, you can project your retirement expenses by putting factors like health, travel, and insurance into consideration. The goal is to spend less than you earn so you can have enough to save for future investments. There are apps and software available out there that can help you track your expenses. Even a good ol' spreadsheet can help get the job done.

**2. Adjust your personal expenses if there is a need to:** As stated earlier, you should strive to be in the *leanFIRE* category, based on retirement spending, because you will have saved at least 25 times your annual expenses. The people in this category spend less than they earn.

**3. Include other sources of income (if any) after your retirement:** If there will be other sources of income, you will need to add them to your overall income. This income could come from *social security pension (for those of us old enough to receive it), employer pensions, stock dividends, interest from bonds, interest from personal loans or crowdfunding sites, annuities* etc.

**4. Profile your retirement rental property:** In this fourth step, the least you should do is estimate the cost, debt structure, and cash-on-cash return for your rental property. You can analyze and calculate the cost and debt structure with your real estate agent and mortgage lenders respectively. For the cash-on-cash return, I recommend that you do not go below 6%, even if it is a free and clear property in a quality location. On the other hand, I also do not recommend going for returns around 15-20%. Although those yields are possible, it is better to build a retirement plan on a more moderate foundation. This part of planning for real estate investment is a curse because of the work involved. However, it is also a blessing, since only a few investors take the pain to do it, leaving you with less competition.

**5. Calculate the amount of money you need to invest with:** Still using the real estate retirement math **(W x r = E) and** Alan as our case study, we already know he has to invest $480,000 at 10% cash-on-cash returns. With this information, figuring out the number of rental properties he can acquire with this money will depend on the property values and debt structure that he chooses. This brings us back to Alan choosing between the *leveraged rental retirement portfolio* and *free and clear retirement portfolio.* If Alan opts for the ***free and clear retirement portfolio***, calculating how many properties $480,000 can buy will be: **Wealth** (capital equity) / **Cost in equity per property** (cost of property). So, if we assume that one rental property costs $60,000, Alan will be able to afford **8** rental **properties ($480,000 / $60,000).** However, if he decides to opt for the ***leveraged rental retirement portfolio*** at 50% leverage, Alan will be able to afford **16 rental properties ($480,000 / $30,000).**

The essence of this step-by-step process was to help you narrow down your financial goals to a specific number of rental properties that you can purchase. Your goals may vary from the example I cited, but I recommend that you try the process for yourself. All I have shared so far will not necessarily give you a precise prediction of your rental income, but you do not have to wait until everything is in perfect order before you start working toward your goals. I hope the information I have shared can help boost your confidence and give you a framework to start with. Good luck!

## SETTING UP A LIMITED LIABILITY COMPANY (LLC) FOR REAL ESTATE INVESTMENT

I am pretty sure the reason you bought this book is either because you have interest in real estate, early retirement, or maybe even both. If at this point, you are certain you want to become a real estate investor and run it as a business, then you should know that having an LLC is a legal entity that real estate investors run for owning properties.

As with any other type of business, there are complexities surrounding real estate investment, and I will recommend them for the following reasons.

- LLCs limit personal liability to potential lawsuits related to the property. In a situation where the owner of a rental property leases it to a tenant whose guest falls over a balcony or down the stairs, it is very likely that the injured guest or tenant would sue the investor based on the unsafe condition of the rental property. Now, if that rental property were owned by a real estate investor individually, they would be named in the lawsuit and have to defend their personal assets from the plaintiff's claims. On the other hand, if that property were owned by an LLC, it would serve as a legal business entity, protecting the investor and leaving only the assets owned by the LLC exposed to potential lawsuits.

- Forming an LLC for your rental property will offer you some significant tax advantages like *pass-through taxation,* which simply means that any income made will pass to the investor (or investors), and taxes are then paid as an individual —the LLC itself does not pay any taxes! This tax treatment will help property investors avoid double taxation (where a corporation is taxed directly on its profits, and owners are then taxed again when they make an income). As a real estate investor, having an LLC also gives you the ability to deduct operating expenses for tax purposes as part of maintaining and managing investment properties. Moreover, based on current IRS rules, the owner of an LLC can deduct mortgage interest the same way that a sole property owner can. It is also noteworthy that the recent changes in the tax law have made some adjustments to how pass-through entities are taxed. Thus, you should discuss whether these changes are to your advantage with your CPA or a professional tax advisor.

- With an LLC, you can create a business bank account or credit card for your investment property to track your expenses, including tax, since they will be deducted from the business account without affecting your personal account.
- LLCs enjoy a greater flexibility than either a corporation or partnership. Although corporations are statutorily required to have officers and directors, the LLC can be managed by its owners or third party managers.
- LLC owners can also easily gift the company's real estate membership interests to their heirs each year. Over time, it will be entirely possible to effectively pass ownership of real estate owned by an LLC to loved ones without having to formally execute and record a new deed. This enables property owners to avoid transfer and recording taxes and fees, which is quite large in many states.
- For investors who own and manage multiple investments, you can use an LLC to protect each investment from liability claims. In simpler words, if someone files a lawsuit against one of your investment properties, it will not affect the others, as long as they are under separate LLCs.

Now that you have seen the benefits of having an LLC for your real estate investment, the real question becomes: *when do I create an LLC for my investments? Before or after buying property?* In my experience, it is best you create an LLC before buying an investment property. Even though property investors can transfer the ownership of properties to an LLC, it is best to create the LLC before making a purchase because it will save you a lot of unnecessary stress, such as that which comes with informing your mortgage holder of the transfer to your LLC. In doing this, a couple of issues can arise, like your mortgage holder wanting to issue another loan with an increased interest rate or close another loan, meaning you will bear the closing cost.

## REASONS WHY REAL ESTATE INVESTORS FAIL

There is no better way to end this chapter than to tell you the reason why real estate investors fail. With all the knowledge you have gleaned thus far, it is imperative that you also recognize why other real estate investors have failed in the past and how you can avoid being another failure statistic.

1. **Taking on too much risk:** Taking too many low down payment deals or buying too many properties too fast can contribute to this potential outcome.
2. **Not educating themselves enough**. Thankfully, you have this book to guide you.
3. **Not doing enough analysis and market research:** Do your retirement math and other calculations.
4. **Not knowing the laws governing real estate investment in their states.**
5. **Not maintaining property up to standards set by the law.**
6. **Giving tenants too much control.**
7. **Poor customer service.**
8. **No business plan/not treating their investment like a business:** This would be not having systems or policies.
9. **Not hiring a team of professionals for their real estate investment.**

## CHAPTER SUMMARY

- In real estate investing, the *buy and hold strategy* is one of the most popular forms of investment. The ***buy and hold strategy*** when an investor buys a property to own over a long period (five to 30 years). The value of that property increases over time, and the investor can enjoy a stable cash flow from the rental income of that property.
- One outstanding benefit of the buy and hold real estate investment strategy is the appreciation of such properties. As long as the property you bought is in a highly sought-after residential area, then the value will continue to appreciate.
- Often, a property will be underpriced because it needs repairs. So, if you plan to buy such a property, make sure the total cost of repairs and the property is still below the market value.

In the next chapter, you will learn how to consider your financing options for real estate investment.

# CHAPTER THREE: CONSIDERING YOUR FINANCING OPTIONS FOR REAL ESTATE INVESTMENT

For many people looking to invest in real estate, the biggest hurdle is not having enough or no money at all to invest. Apart from having the money to invest with, another problem is knowing how much you actually need to invest in real estate. In this chapter, I will teach you how you can still invest in real estate, even if you don't have a lot of money. But first, let us start with the major expenses you will make when investing in real estate.

1. Purchase price
2. Down payment
3. Repairs
4. Maintenance

Let's see how you can manage the money you have for real estate investment effectively as we consider each expense category listed above.

## PURCHASE PRICE

The lower the price of a property, the less money you will need to buy it. However, people tend to buy rental properties in the same standards—and even location—as they would want to live in personally. You think there's nothing wrong with this, right? Let me show you why there is *everything* wrong with this.

Something you must know when buying rental properties for real estate investment is that the considerations you take when buying a rental property are *not* the same as when you are looking for a home. Your rental property is not all about you or what you want, so it must not be close to your work—it doesn't need to be in your preferred school district or have the fancy granite countertops and wood floors you've always wanted. Rather, your rental property needs *to make money for you.*

People are conditioned to believe that bigger is better, more expensive is better, and so on. But that's not true. Affordable houses appreciate faster, generate more cash flow, and are less affected during economic downturns. It is better to own several small houses than one big one because it diversifies your risks and makes it easier for you to sell one and not the whole thing, in case you need quick cash.

Some investors' strategy is to buy two houses, pay down the loans for 15 years, then sell one and use the proceeds to pay off the other. In this case, you will have a free and clear house in half the time with cash flow you can live on. Although the equity you own is the same, it's better to own a whole house in 15 years than half a house.

Here are three simple tips to keep in mind about property prices:

- **Buy a property around the median price:** If you wrote down all the rental properties sold from the least to most expensive, the median price will be the one directly in the middle. Then, the next thing to do is set your initial purchase price range to include houses between 50% under the median to 25% above it. Any property that is lower than 50% of the median is probably in high-crime areas that take a lot more time and stress to manage, and that which will also require more cash for surprises, like having your AC unit stolen overnight. On the other hand, any property higher than 25% over median means your mortgage payment will probably be so high that your cash flow will be weak. Plus, it will be harder to find tenants willing to rent at such a high price.
- **Do a comparative analysis:** Once you find a property you like, you'll want to do a comparative real estate analysis. You would do this by finding out how much similar rental properties in the area sold for over the past several months. To make sure the comparisons are accurate, look for properties with the same number of bedrooms and bathrooms. Once you find several similar properties, study their selling prices, as they will give you a good idea of what you should pay when you begin the negotiation process for the property you want.
- **Negotiate:** People forget that house prices are not set in stone, and unless you are in a really hot market, it does not hurt to make a lower offer.

However, before you try to negotiate, make sure you know your numbers because you should be able to support your lesser offer with facts and statistics rather than just a "gut feeling." You should also be willing to walk away from your choice investment property if the need arises because many sellers will be emotionally attached to their properties and unwilling to compromise. They may also have an unrealistic idea of what their home is worth, especially if it just went on the market. If a homeowner is not willing to consider your offer, hold off on purchasing. You can always keep in touch with them every couple of weeks to see if they have had a change of heart and are willing to bargain again. Negotiating might be rather stressful, but it is worth your time if you want to get a better purchase price. For instance, negotiating gives you the opportunity to save as much as $5,000 or even more, which will, in turn, also lower the down payment.

## DOWN PAYMENT

As with the purchase price, the less the down payment you have to make on a property, the better. The more leverage you have when borrowing to buy your investment property, the less cash out-of-pocket will be needed and the higher your cash-on-cash return. To explain further, analyze these two scenarios and choose the one that looks better to you when purchasing a $100,000 property and getting a loan with a 6.5% interest rate:

1. Put down $20,000 with a mortgage payment of $505 and own one property.

2. Put down $10,000 with a mortgage payment of $568 and have more money available to buy a second property.

If your guess is option 2, you are correct! Did you notice that the difference in mortgage payment was only $63/month? Even if you pay a little extra per month, as long as your rental income covers the amount, then you will be much closer to repeating the process and having twice the benefits of property ownership.

Some people would choose the lower payment, but by doing so, they are tying up all their cash in one house. Personally, I would rather buy two houses and a put $10,000 down payment on each than $20,000 on one house. Buy rental property in a market that is set for long-term and has stable growth and get as much leverage as you can.

The best way to do a down payment for a rental property is through "house hacking." This means getting an owner-occupied loan (as low as 3.5% down with FHA) instead of a loan meant for real estate investors (usually 10%). Don't try to outsmart the system—just follow the guidelines that state you must make the house your personal residence for at least one year. Now, you may have to put off buying your dream home for a year to live in this one, but 12 months down the line, you'll have enough cash on hand to do it again because you didn't tie it all up in one big down payment.

Some investors buy duplexes or fourplexes using FHA loans, and then live in one unit while renting out the rest. The income from the other units compensates or even covers their own housing payment. But, even if you do not like the idea of house hacking, just remember that less money as a down payment is usually better, and 10% down is still better than tying up 20% or more. The reason is that, in addition to the down payment, you will have closing costs, title company fees, lender fees, loan escrows, first year's insurance, a property inspection, and the deed preparation fee.

Finally, you can get what is called a *good faith estimate* from your mortgage broker to gain a more streamlined idea for your rental property location and loan type. But with a rough estimate, expect it to be about 3.5% of the purchase price.

## REPAIRS AND MAINTENANCE

That you have successfully bought a rental property does not mean you won't still spend more money on it. As I stated in chapter two, it is near impossible to find a rental property that will require absolutely no repairs at all. However, the best you can do is make sure the repairs are not major but minor fixes. It will take money to maintain a property and keep it in rentable condition. How much these repairs and the maintenance will cost depends on two things:

1. The initial work needed to get it rentable.
2. The average annual maintenance costs.

## EXPENSES FOR REPAIR WORK

You will need to factor in a repair budget for items like paint, carpet, counters, cabinets, appliances, and anything else needed to make it liveable. However, if these things do not require fixing in the rental property you buy, then you are in luck. Bear in mind that while making repairs, your rental property does not have to look as great as a house you are trying to sell. You can get away with linoleum counters instead of granite, white appliances instead of stainless steel, and you can repaint old cabinets rather than install fancy new ones.

If you spend a lot of money fixing stuff in your rental property, you will rarely get your money back from the extra investments; if renters want that perfect house so badly, they can go buy one themselves. You may also need to have enough cash to cover any holding costs on hand, like mortgage payments, property insurance, and taxes for one to two months while you are fixing it up and finding a new tenant.

## AVERAGE ANNUAL MAINTENANCE COSTS

These costs are not as urgent as repair costs. But if you do not take care of them now, you may find yourself paying more later on, or in the worst case scenario, stuck with a house you cannot rent. Some things you will need to keep money aside for every year, or as the need arises, include cleaning the gutters or investing in a new roof.

Two important people to count on before you make your purchase are your property inspector and handyman. The property inspector will help you spot subtle areas requiring repair that you may miss, while your handyman can help you get estimates of the repairs needed.

It is important to factor in vacancies and other unexpected costs when buying a rental property. Although some landlords can boast about having the same tenant for years, the truth is that everyone will not be so fortunate. Thus, until you replace tenants who move out, it will be you paying the mortgage, giving it a fresh coat of paint, and fixing any other items needed to get it in rentable shape again. But the good news is, when you allow good tenants in, the cost of repairs will not come as frequently as they would, especially when they maintain your property well.

Finally, it is better to overestimate your repair and maintenance costs rather than underestimate them. If you believe you will need to hold back on repairs or reserves—or worse, pray for good luck—it will be better that you forget about buying a rental property and save until you can afford to pay for repairs.

## HOW TO BUY RENTAL PROPERTY BELOW MARKET VALUE (BMV)

Below Market Value (BMV) properties are residential properties available for sale at a price that is below their actual market value. There are several reasons why a property would be put up for sale below its market value, and as a real estate investor, it will be your duty to take advantage of these reasons, which are listed below.

1. Separation or divorce.
2. Death in the family.
3. Job relocation.
4. Financial distress (job loss, pay cut, medical condition).
5. Property requires updating, extensive renovation, or it is in mid-construction.
6. Partnership dispute.
7. Foreclosed bank-owned property.
8. Motivated sellers (check properties that have been on sale for a long time).

## HOW TO USE LEVERAGE TO BUY RENTAL PROPERTIES

Having learned how you can buy a rental property below market value, I'll now teach you how to use leverage to buy rental properties. Leverage is defined as using borrowed capital for an investment, expecting the profits made to be greater than the interest payable. Knowing how to use leverage is important because after seeing the opportunities you have to buy a rental property below market value, you will still need money to buy it.

Using myself as an example, when I buy a rental property, I always get a loan which allows me to increase my returns. If you can afford to buy a property without taking a loan, then please do. Otherwise, here is a quick example of how leverage can increase returns on rental properties for an investor.

- Purchase price: $100,000
- Monthly rent: $1,300
- Expenses: $430
- *Cash flow without a loan: $870*

To make things simple, we will assume that you are the investor and have to pay out $110,000 after closing costs and repairs to get this property ready to rent. The return on your money would be 9.5% which is the ***cash flow without return multiplied by 12 months and divided by total cost of the rental property*** ($870*12/$110,000).

However, if you get a loan on this property with 20% down at 4.5%, the payment would be a little over $400. That would leave $470 in cash flow each month, which would equal a return of 17.6% ($470*12/$32,000). To get the $30,000 cash needed with the loan, I added the $10,000 we used for the cash deal for repairs and closing costs, and then I added another $2,000 for the costs associated with getting the loan, plus the 20% down payment.

Can you see how much higher the return is when you use leverage? Now, not only does leveraging your money with rental properties provide a better return, but it also comes with other benefits:

- Every month, you pay down your mortgage by a certain amount and increase your equity.
- Rent appreciation and property value appreciation will increase your returns significantly because you used less cash.
- By only spending $32,000 instead of $110,000, you can buy three properties instead of just one. This amplifies the other benefits of rentals: tax advantages, mortgage pay down, rent appreciation, and property value appreciation.

The following loans offer lower down payment: FHA—3.5% down, USDA/VA—0% down (if you buy as an owner occupant). But they have a higher monthly payment and require mortgage insurance.

## HOW TO COVER REAL ESTATE PAYMENT WITH NO MONEY DOWN

What if you do not have any money at all and still want to invest in real estate? Getting loans from traditional lenders, like a bank or credit union, requires a down payment of 20% or more of the purchase, which can sum up to tens of thousands of dollars.

When someone says they are buying real estate with *no money down,* they are referring to putting very little or no money of their own into the investment upfront. Some real estate investors even use other people's money for a down payment or creative financing options to eliminate the down payment altogether, thereby putting very little or none of their own money into the real estate investment. The less money you invest in a property, the higher the likelihood of increased returns (see the analysis above).

That is why knowledgeable real estate investors use a

couple of the following methods to reduce how much they put into an investment.

- House hunting.
- Seller financing: making monthly payments to the seller, which works well with motivated sellers.
- Assume seller's existing mortgage.
- Rent to own: lease with the option to purchase.
- Real estate partnerships: partner to finance deal.
- Home equity loan: using existing equity in your home.
- Hard money loans: short-term loans (should be paid within a fixed duration).
- Private money lenders or peer-to-peer lenders.
- Trade something other than cash.
- Your 401(k), as long as you return it within 60 days, or borrow from a 401(k) administrator.
- Roth IRA: you can pull contributions (not earnings) any time, penalty-free, through this option.
- Self-directed IRA to pay a down payment.

## HOW TO FINANCE YOUR RENTAL PROPERTY INVESTMENT

If, on the other hand, you have some money to invest in real estate, the next question should be, *How do I pay for my rental property investment?* This question might seem unnecessary, but there is a lot to learn in terms of paying for a real estate investment. There are various options to choose from:

1. **Pay all cash:** The king of all financing tactics is the all-cash deal. Remember that cash is king, even in real estate. If there are two offers for a seller to consider, and one is all-cash and

the other is using conventional financing, the seller will usually go with the all-cash deal. This is because cash is quick, clean, and there are no banks to deal with that could impede closing the sale. The all-cash deal is very attractive to sellers because it's the easiest form of financing tactics available. However, it is not the best way to get your ROI. As I stated earlier, using leverage (loans) will give you a higher ROI because the less you put down for a property, the higher your ROI will be.

**2. Conventional mortgages:** Using mortgage on a property will mean getting a loan from a bank that will pay the purchase price, excluding the down payment you put toward the property. For example, if you buy a rental property for $100,000 and put $10,000 down, the loan you will have is $90,000, and you will make payments every single month until that money is paid off and the bank gets interest on what they lent you. Most conventional mortgages for an investment property will require a minimum of 20% down payment, and some can even ask for 25% to 30%, depending on the lender you are working with. Conventional mortgages usually have the lowest interest rate of most of the financing options available. There are many term lengths to choose from: 10 years, 15 years, 20 years, and 30 years. The longer the term, the more money you will pay in total interest, but the lower your payments will be. In the beginning, only 15% or so of your monthly payment will go toward the principal, and 85% will go to interest.

**3. Portfolio loans:** This is an alternative to conventional mortgages. A portfolio loan is a loan kept in-house by the lender, rather than bundled and sold to a large mortgage servicing company. Examples include local community banks and online investment property lenders. These loans typically require at least a 20% down payment, which is to be settled within 14-30 days, and they are more collateral-oriented in their underwriting. This means they analyze your deal and the property carefully to make sure it is a good deal, but they also have fewer requirements regarding your income, and they often do not require income documentation. Another advantage with portfolio loans is that many portfolio lenders do not impose seasoning requirements or ban people from borrowing the down payment. On the flip side, however, is that portfolio lenders charge slightly higher interest rates and shorter payment terms and up-front fees, even though they are relatively easy to work with, since they require far less documentation than conventional mortgage lenders.

**4. Home loans and home equity line of credit (HELOC):** If you currently own a rental property, you may have equity accumulation on the property, which you can use to purchase more rental properties. A home equity loan rarely exceeds 80% of the value of your rental property, meaning you can borrow up to 80% the value of a rental property, but if you have enough equity on the property, it can be an excellent way to purchase more rentals. For example, assuming you own a home worth $200,000, and you owe $70,000, you could borrow up to 80% of the $200,000, minus the original note of $70,000. That means you can borrow up to $90,000 from your equity. A good way to use this loan would be to purchase a $90,000 property (including repairs and maintenance) that will make you money each month from the rent and use that money to pay the mortgage each month. Here's an example: a mortgage payment of $90,000 may be around $650 a month, and you can buy a property that rents for $1000, giving you a profit of $350 monthly cash flow. A home equity line of credit (HELOC) is similar to an equity loan, but the only difference is that a HELOC is a revolving line of credit, similar to a credit card. With a HELOC, you can borrow money against the equity on your home and then pay it off, so you won't incur any interest if the balance is zero. The annual fees that you incur having a HELOC are nothing compared to the value that it brings to have money at your fingertips and ready for the next deal.

**5. Cash-out refinance:** A cash-out refinance comes with a fixed-rate, but it may extend the life of your existing mortgage. A longer loan term could mean paying more interest for the primary residence, which would be weighed against the expected returns that an investment property would bring in.

Now that we've gone over the different options available to finance your rental property investment, it is important that you consider each of them carefully before choosing the one that suits you best. If taking an investment loan appeals to you the most, then you should know what to look for exactly when taking one.

## WHAT TO LOOK FOR IN AN INVESTMENT LOAN (LEVERAGE)

**1. Interest rate:** Loans with high interest rates are short-term and used when a deal needs to be closed quickly. If you plan to accept a loan with a high interest rate, make sure you can make the payments.

***How to Lower Your Interest Rate***

- Maintain a good credit score.
- Have a consistent work history.

- Shop around for the best rates.
- Ask your bank to lower your rate—research the market rates, talk to the right people, make your case, call their bluffs, and use a broker for refinancing.
- Put more money down.
- Shorten your loan.
- Set up automatic mortgage payments.
- Refinance.

**2. Loan terms:** For loans with balloon payments, you should be confident that you will pay the balance when it is due.

*NB: A balloon payment is the lump sum payment attached to a loan, mortgage, or commercial loan. The investor would usually make this payment toward the end of the loan period. Balloon payments are higher than what you might pay toward the loan on a monthly basis.*

**3. Prepayment penalties:** If you think you may sell or refinance the property with a prepayment penalty, factor that into your costs.

4. Check all the fees to determine how much money you will need to close and how much the loan will be for.

5. Loan conditions that require, for example, that you earn a minimum amount or a certain amount be paid into an escrow for major repairs.

## RISKS INVOLVED WITH USING LEVERAGE

1. **General market risk:** As an investor, you cannot control the shocks that will hit real estate investment, but you can control it by diversifying your portfolio.

2. **Asset-level risk:** In real estate investing, there will always be demand for apartments in both good and bad economies, so multi-family real estate is considered low-risk, and therefore, often yields lower returns.

3. **Idiosyncratic risk:** This includes construction (in a case where rent cannot be collected during the specified time), the location of a property, and environmental risks. Idiosyncratic risks are defined as specific to the asset and its business plan.

4. **Liquidity risk:** This is basically how easy it is for an investor to get ROI for their investment on a property. A couple of factors are responsible for this risk, but the bottom line is in buying a property with high cash flow potential.

5. **Credit risk:** The length and stability of the property's income stream will determine its value. A property leased to a Fortune 500 company for 30 years will command a much higher price than a multi-tenant office building with similar rent. However, keep in mind that even the most creditworthy tenants can go bankrupt, as history has shown us over and again.

6. **Replacement cost risk:** This risk is associated with newer and more modern rental properties entering the market, which will make yours less desirable to tenants. Analyzing

this situation calls for understanding a property's replacement cost to know if it is economically possible for a new property to come along and steal away those tenants. To estimate the replacement cost, consider a property's asset class, location, and sub-market in that location. This will help investors know if rent can rise high enough to make new construction viable.

7. **Structural risk:** This relates to the investment's financial structure and the rights it provides to individual participants. Structural risk also exists in joint ventures. In these types of deals, the investor has to be aware of their rights relative to their position in the LLC, which is either a majority or minority holding. This will dictate the compensation they will have to pay the manager of the LLC when a property is sold.

## DON'TS IN USING LEVERAGE

1. Counting on high levels of appreciation.
2. Ending up with a monthly payment.
3. Buying an overpriced property (or property that is cheap but cannot fetch you good monthly rent) which will lead to poor cash flow.
4. Forgetting that cash flow is king.

In conclusion, be thorough when investigating an investment property and do not be afraid to walk away from a deal if you are uncertain whether it will cover the loan payments. You also should not be afraid to turn down a loan offer if you are not comfortable with the terms. With the right deals and loan terms, leveraging real estate can help you invest in real estate in different ways and allow you to diversify your portfolio. Knowing what leverage in real estate is, what it can do for you, and how it can work against you will help you make sure you are maximizing what your money will do for you.

## CHAPTER SUMMARY

- As with the purchase price, the less your down payment on a property, the better. The more leverage you have when borrowing money for your investment property, the less cash-out-of-pocket is needed and the higher your cash-on-cash return will be.
- The best way to do down payment for a rental property is through "house hacking." This means getting an owner-occupied loan (as low as 3.5% down with FHA) instead of a loan meant for real estate investors (usually 10%).
- Bear in mind that while making repairs, your rental property does not have to look as pretty as a house you are trying to sell.

In the next chapter, you will learn how to assess and select a rental property for investment.

# CHAPTER FOUR: ASSESSING AND SELECTING A RENTAL PROPERTY

In a previous chapter, I made it clear that when buying a rental property, you should not consider the usual things that you would when buying a property for yourself. All that should concern you is the ability of the rental property to make money for you. I also said that spending more than you need to on a rental property is a waste because affordable houses appreciate faster, generate more cash flow, and are less affected by economic downturns. Thus, it is better to own several small houses than one big one to diversify your risk.

## WHAT TO LOOK AT WHEN LOOKING FOR A RENTAL PROPERTY

1. **Condition of the property:** There is no perfect house out there; however, you must make sure you do not spend too much on repairs, especially any major ones. You also need to consider the time it will take to fix the rental property because the house will be vacant during the repairs and you will have to cover expenses, such as taxes.

**2. The 1% rule:** Income should be 1% of price; for example, if you buy a rental property for $100,000, it would need to bring in $1,000 a month. This amount is determined by a simple math equation: estimated monthly rent divided by the price of the house ($1,000/$100,000 = 1%). The only way you can consider buying a house that does not meet the 1% rule is if the property is in a neighborhood that is rapidly changing and improving, with home values and rents estimated to jump significantly over a short amount of time.

**3. Property taxes:** High taxes will eat into your profits, whereas low taxes will allow you to keep a large amount of your rental income. Some locations charge investors higher taxes than owner-occupants, so it would be wise to call your local tax assessor to determine if this is the case. Also, remember that even if you find the perfect house in the perfect neighborhood, high property taxes could still make it a poor investment choice.

**4. Insurance costs:** Just like property taxes, insurance costs can eat into your profits. The first step is deciding on the kind of coverage you want for the investment property. The next thing to consider will be the location of the property, since some flood, earthquake, or disaster prone areas could have higher premiums, meaning that the investment may not be worth it. Once this is settled, compare insurance costs and choose the one that's most suited to your needs.

**5. The neighborhood:** How safe a neighborhood is will determine how much you will have to spend in securing your property, the number of tenant applications you will get, and even the cost of monthly rent. It makes sense that tenants who will take the risk of living in an unsafe or fairly safe neighborhood will not want to pay an expensive rent. If your rental property is for a family and located near a school district, you can be sure that many families will apply to live in your property because it is favorable to them.

**6. Property management:** Being a landlord can be a headache at times, so you should consider whether you are willing to deal with 3 a.m. phone calls when there is a plumbing disaster. Many investors choose to hire a property management company to take care of everything for them, and they charge around 10% of the monthly rent, along with a fee for procuring tenants. Some also charge to supervise maintenance repairs from outside vendors. Although some landlords believe that the management fee is worth it, there are others who choose to save money and deal with problems on their own. This decision is purely a personal one, but one you should consider carefully.

7. **Know the risks:** As with all things in real estate, buying an investment property is not without its risks. Some of the most significant ones to keep in mind include:

a. Not having the rental interest that you anticipate.
b. Having to front for expensive repairs.
c. Property taxes going up.
d. The local market economy changing.
e. Bad tenants, resulting in repair or even eviction costs.

Do not focus on the risks alone; if that is what everyone did, no one would ever buy an investment property. However, you shouldn't ignore them either. No investment is ever a guarantee—you just need to make sure you are not blindsided if something goes wrong, and that you have some flexibility worked into your finances. An investment property can be one of the most fruitful purchases that you ever make. To get this result, work with an experienced advisor who can help you navigate the process and make the best purchase possible. Also, be sure to evaluate all of the factors above thoroughly to ensure that the investment you make is a smart one.

## EVALUATING A REAL ESTATE INVESTMENT

When evaluating a rental property for a real estate investment, there is so much research that you must do, and I will show you how to do it rather than just giving you a list of things you should look out for when buying rental property.

1. **The neighborhood/rental market:** It is good to know how real estate is performing in a city, but such would not give you the most accurate data. Every city consists of several local housing markets, and some are better than others for real estate investing. Therefore, the first step of a rental market analysis is evaluating and assessing the neighborhood. Investors should always verify that the neighborhood where they want to buy a property is not only good, but also desirable. There are specific things that attract good renters to a certain area, which will also help your investment property appreciate.

- Price-to-income ratio—Compare median house price to median household income.
- Price-to-rent ratio—Compare median home prices to median rents in the market. If high, not a good investment opportunity.
- Evaluate the neighborhood—Access to public transport, high walkability score, good local school rating, nearby amenities and attractions, easy access to dining and shopping, and open businesses. Avoid noisy areas, places where there

are a lot of permanently closed businesses, streets are not cared for, and multiple properties on the street are distressed or vacant.
- Housing inventory or supply in the market, specifically of your type of property. Too much supply can be a red flag.
- Demand for rental properties. A 35/65 percent ratio of renter to homeowner.
- Opportunity for future growth in the neighborhood—for example, new infrastructure or developments and employment growth.
- Vacancy rates in the area.
- Current real estate market and economy—This refers to the cycle in the market you are in.

2. **Property:** This is one of the most important things to evaluate because you cannot change the location of a property, so you will want to make sure it is in a safe and desirable area. An instance would be you buying a family rental property in a college area. There are many benefits to buying an income property near a college because there will always be new students looking for housing. Since the students' parents often pay the rent, you might be able to charge a higher rent because of the desirability of the area and increased demand for apartments. Apart from the location, there are other things to look out for:

- Rent per square foot—Compare to the average rent per square foot in the neighborhood to see if they have good rental potential.
- Net operating income—Rent minus all expenses.
- Gross rental yield—Annual rent / Total Property Cost (including closing and renovation).
- Capitalization rate / annual net rental yield—This

formula is used to estimate potential return on investment. Annual rent and annual expenses divided by total property cost.
- Cash Flow—Note if your rent can cover the mortgage payment, taxes, insurance, and operating expenses; this is important because it is what you will be making in retirement, plus inflation.
- Cash on Cash Return—Annual cash flow / total cash invested (aim for 15%).
- Price/Earnings Ratio—This is the market value of the property divided by the current net operating income.

3. **Resale value of the property:** For example, a clean bathroom and strong roof would be more valuable than an inground pool and TV screening room.

4. **Property location:** Distance to necessities and the type of tenant it would attract.

## HOW TO VALUE RENTAL PROPERTIES

To value a rental property means to determine how much the rental property will yield as rent for an investor. There are five ways to value rental properties and they are:

1. **Sales Comparison Approach (SCA):** This is the most recognizable form of evaluating residential rental properties, and it is used by real estate agents and appraisers. This approach is a comparison of similar homes that have been sold or rented locally over a period. SCA depends on attributes or features (such as the number of bedrooms and bathrooms, garages and/or driveways, pools, decks, and fireplaces) or anything that makes a property unique and

noteworthy to assign a relative price value. For example, if a 2,000-square-foot townhouse is renting for $1/square foot, investors can reasonably approximate their income, provided comparable townhouses in the area are going for that too. However, it is important to note that SCA is generic and should be the baseline for the value of a property and not a prediction tool because each property has its unique features, and the tastes of investors will differ from one another. A 2,000 square feet apartment with a garage, swimming pool, six bedrooms, and five full bathrooms cannot be the baseline for valuing another property with half the number of bedrooms and no pool and is only 1,200 square feet.

**2. Capital Asset Pricing Model (CAPM):** This is a more comprehensive valuation method than the SCA. It introduces the concepts of risk and opportunity cost as it applies to real estate investing. CAPM compares potential return on investment from rental income with no-risk investments. Not all rental properties are the same; location and property age are important things to consider when valuing a property. Renting older property will mean landlords will likely incur higher maintenance expenses, whereas property for rent in a high-crime area will likely require more safety precautions than a rental in a gated community. The CAPM model factors in these risks before considering your investment or establishing a rental pricing structure. In summary, this model can help you determine what return you deserve for putting your money at risk.

**3. Income Approach:** This approach relies on determining the annual capitalization rate for an investment. This rate is the projected annual income from the gross rent multiplier divided by the current value of the property. Say for instance, an office building costs $120,000 to purchase, and the expected monthly income from rentals is $1,200; the expected annual capitalization rate is: $14,400 **($1,200 x 12 months) ÷ $120,000 = 0.12 or** 12%. Also, future rental incomes may be more or less valuable five years from now than they are today especially due to inflation.

**4. Gross Rent Multiplier Approach (GRM):** Values a rental property based on the amount of rent an investor can collect each year. It is an easy way to determine whether a property is worth the investment before considering any taxes, insurance, utilities, and other associated expenses, so it should be taken with a grain of salt. Although it may be similar to the income approach, the GRM approach does not use net operating income as its cap rate; rather, it uses gross rent. The gross rent multiplier's cap rate is greater than one, whereas the cap rate for the income approach is a percentage value. In order to get an accurate comparison, you should compare the GRMs and rental income of similar properties to the one in which you are interested. Let us assume a commercial property is sold for $500,000 with an annual income of $90,000. To calculate its GRM, divide the sale price by the annual rental income: **$500,000 / $90,000 = 5.56.** You can compare this figure to another property you are considering, as long as you know its annual rental income. You can also figure out its market value by multiplying the GRM by its annual income. If the market value is higher than the one that sold recently—i.e. for $500,000—it may not be worth it, so consider moving on.

**5. Cost Approach:** This is done by combining land value and depreciated value of improvements. Appraisers who use this method often adopt the highest and best use to summarize the cost approach to real property. It is also frequently used as a basis for valuing vacant land. For example, if you are an apartment developer looking to purchase three acres of land in a barren area to convert into condominiums, the value of that land will be based on the best use of that land. If the land is surrounded by oil fields and the nearest person lives 20 miles away, the best use and therefore highest value of that property is not converting it to apartments, but possibly expanding drilling rights to find more oil. Another best use argument has to do with property zoning. If the prospective property is not zoned for residential purposes, its value is reduced, since the developer will incur significant costs to get it rezoned. The cost approach method is considered most reliable when used on newer structures and less reliable for older properties.

There is no perfect way to value a rental property. What most serious investors do is look at components from all of these valuation methods before making an investment decision. Knowing these introductory valuation concepts should be a step in the right direction to getting into the real estate investment game. Once you have found a property that can yield you a favorable income, calculate the interest rate for your new property using a mortgage calculator. This tool will also give you more concrete figures to work with when evaluating a prospective rental property.

## HOW TO ESTIMATE RENTAL RATES

1. If the rental property is already rented, get the rental history from the owner.
2. If vacant or owner-occupied, check rental listings for comparable properties, ask a local property

manager, or get a rental appraisal done to determine the worth of the property.

3. Comparable properties should have a similar location, square feet, number of bedrooms and bathrooms, lot size, condition, amenities, and days on market.
4. **Cap rate:** The cap rate is the expected annual return on investment. It is calculated as a ratio between the net income *(**annual rental income minus expenses**)* and the market value of the property. It shows the rate of return on a rental property that you can expect in the first year.
5. **Demand:** During a bad economy, the demand for rentals goes down, since only a few people can afford rent. At this time, rental property owners have to reduce the price of the rent that the tenant has to pay.
6. **Expenses made:** The repairs or maintenance done on a rental property also determines the rate. This is why it is so important not to spend too much on repairs so you can charge affordable rent. Or better yet, buy a property that doesn't require too many (major) repairs that will cost you a fortune.

## FACTORS THAT CAN AFFECT RENTAL RATE

1. **Amenities.**
2. **Occupancy and vacancy rates:** Occupancy rate is a metric that shows the share of months booked versus all available (months) for a rental, while vacancy rate stands for the nights you would not be earning a rental income. It is about 30% on average for short-term rentals, 45% for vacation

homes, and 5% for single-family, long-term rentals.

With this information on hand, let us observe a practical example of estimating rent. Let's assume the following:

*Desired net rental income = $500*
*Property tax = $100*
*Insurance = $75*
*Maintenance = $50*
*Average vacancy rate for rental comps in your area = 5%*
*Financing costs = $500*
*$100 + $75 + $50 + $500 = $725 in expenses*

You will need this much to cover your costs, but that is not all. Adding the desired profit on a rental property of $500 means you will need to charge at least $1,225. But the rental vacancy rate means 5% of the time, you would not be earning rental income. We suggest that you add 5% to the rental rate to cover for vacancies.

*1.05 x $1,225 = $1,286*

This is the answer to the question, *How much should I charge for rent?* in this particular example.

## ESTIMATING REHABILITATION COSTS AND EXPENSES

**Rehab Costs:** By understanding how much it will cost to rehab a property, you can determine your maximum allowable offer and avoid paying too much for the property. The question to ask yourself is, *Do I want a property that requires only cosmetic repairs, or am I willing to do some work, like new* *plumbing, floors, etc?* Also, consider labor costs, or if you can do the repairs yourself, write down the problems in each part of the property and condense your list into 25 categories. Once this is done, determine a rehab price for each category by asking a local contractor for help on a more accurate calculation.

**Operating expenses:** Includes your mortgage payment, utilities to be shouldered by the landlord (find out from the previous landlord or check previous bills), property management (8-12% of rent), HOA fees, property taxes, pest control, lawn maintenance, vacancy allowance (5% of rent), and other maintenance items (5-10% of rent).

Once you get your realistic property price and rental and expense forecasts, run various scenarios (best, normal, and worst-case). For example, if rents decrease for five years at a pace of 5% a year, will you be okay? If mortgage rates for 30-year fixed loans increase from 3.5% to 5% in five years, what will happen to the demand? If the principal value declines another 20%, will you jump off a bridge? Always run bearish, realistic, and bullish case scenarios as your bare minimum to be on the safe side.

## CHAPTER SUMMARY

- Spending more than you need to on a rental property is a waste because affordable houses appreciate faster, generate more cash flow, and are less affected in an economic downturn. Thus, it is better to own several small houses than one big one to diversify your risk.
- There is no perfect house out there; however, you must make sure you do not spend too much on repairs, especially major ones. You also need to

consider the time it will take to fix the rental property because the house will be vacant during the repairs and you will have to cover expenses, like taxes.

- If you buy a rental property for $100,000, it would need to bring in $1,000 a month. This amount is determined by a simple math equation: estimated monthly rent divided by the price of the house ($1,000/$100,000 = 1%).

In the next chapter, you will learn how to make an offer.

# CHAPTER FIVE: MAKE AN OFFER

Once you have run the numbers and determined a good property to invest in and the maximum price you are willing to pay; it is time to make your offer. This is where things get serious, and you will need to prepare the paperwork and purchase offer. A purchase offer is a legal document that outlines the price an investor will pay for the home and other key terms of the transaction. For a real estate investor, putting together a strong purchase offer is the single most important step to buying an investment property. It is what will determine whether you will become the new property owner or start your property search all over again.

In order to get a good real estate deal, you will need to know how much to offer on a house because you do not want to overpay. As a general rule in real estate investing, the less money you pay up front, the higher the ROI. However, if you offer a cheap price, you risk having the seller write you off completely. So, how can you make sure your offer will be the one the seller cannot refuse? The answer to this is striking the right balance, where both you (the investor) and the seller get what you want. Given the size and long-term implications of this buying process, it is in your best interest as a first-time real estate investor to understand the following fully when making an offer:

1. What a purchase offer letter contains.
2. How to determine the best offer price.
3. When you should offer below the asking price.
4. How to craft the best offer.

## WHAT TO INCLUDE IN AN OFFER LETTER

Making an offer on a house is not just about telling the seller how much you are willing to pay for it. Typically, a purchase offer comprises the following key components:

1. **Consideration window:** This specifies how long the offer's terms remain valid (i.e. how long the seller has to consider it). If the seller fails to respond by the end of the consideration window, the buyer (investor) will be free to make another offer.

2. **Earnest money deposit:** This should be indicated in the offer and a personal or cashier's check in the document. It shows that you're serious about purchasing the house and may be anywhere between 1% and 3% of the total purchase price.

3. **Description of property:** This is a legal description of the physical property, as written on the original title. It should comprise a combination of the subdivision name, block and lot numbers, property's numerical measurements, and descriptions of its physical boundaries.

**4. Total purchase price and financing:** This states the total price that you are willing to pay for the property and the financing method (such as a conventional loan or FHA mortgage). It also describes the financing method, down payment amount, amount to be financed, loan terms, and interest rate.

**5. Description of included fixtures and appliances:** This describes the fixtures, appliances, mechanical items, personal property, and other *appurtenances* to be included in the property's sale at no additional cost. The most common examples include kitchen appliances and HVAC equipment.

**6. Closing costs:** Specifies who is responsible for closing costs and what amounts. For example, you might request that the seller pay $3,000 toward closing costs, with you being responsible for the balance.

**7. Contingencies:** These are conditions that the seller should agree to if they accept your offer and want the real estate deal to carry on. Common contingencies include home inspection, hazard inspection, appraisal, financing, sewer and well inspection, title, and walk-through contingencies.

**8. Closing and delivery dates:** Stipulates the closing date or day the transaction is finalized. It also stipulates when the home is to be delivered by the seller to the buyer (i.e. when the buyer can move in).

**9. Arbitration agreement/disclosure:** This is an optional addendum that, when signed by the buyer and seller, both parties agree to settle all disputes through binding arbitration and waive their rights to a court trial.

## TIPS ABOUT PURCHASE PRICE

**1. Buy around the median price:** If you listed all the homes sold from least to most expensive, the median price will be the one directly in the middle. Now, set your initial price range to include houses between 50% under the median to 25% over it.

**2. Do a comparative real estate analysis/sales comparison approach:** You can do this by finding out how much similar properties in the area sold for over the past several months. To make sure the comparisons are valid, look for homes with about the same number of bedrooms and bathrooms. Once you have identified several similar properties, take a look at their selling prices. These prices will give you a good idea of what you should pay when you start negotiating.

**3. Always negotiate, but make sure you know your numbers:** You should be able to support the lesser figure you are offering with facts and statistics rather than just a gut feeling. Also, be prepared to walk away from an investment property because you *might* have to. The reason is that sometimes, sellers are emotionally attached to their properties and unwilling to compromise. They also may have an unrealistic idea of what their home is worth, especially if it has just entered the market.

**4. When you can make a lowball offer (maximum of 15% of listing price):** A lowball offer means offering less than what you think the property is worth. When buying an investment property, investors want to save money, so they go in with a lowball offer. However, this is not always the right move because it could start you off on the wrong foot with the seller, or you may wind up without the home you want. I'm not saying you should *not* do it because, sometimes, a lowball offer will benefit both the buyer and seller. But making a lowball offer will depend on the circumstances more than the investment property itself. Here are a few scenarios where making a lowball offer would make sense:

- The seller wants out.
- The property has been on the market for a while.
- The property requires updates.
- The property is obviously overpriced.

## CONSIDERATIONS WHEN MAKING YOUR OFFER PRICE

**1. Housing market's condition (seller's vs buyer's market):** The first thing that first-time real estate investors should remember is that they should not believe the initial price tag on a property because it is the market that decides. This means that the best offer you can make on a house will depend on the current market conditions (if it is a buyer's or seller's market). If there are a lot of similar houses up for sale and are staying on the market for longer than a month, then you are in a buyer's market ***(high inventory, low demand)***. On the other hand, a seller's market is where the ***demand is high but inventory is low.*** In such markets, homes could go into contract within a week or two of being listed. Sometimes, sellers take advantage of this and list their houses at a low price. Seems counteractive, right? But it is a strategy that some sellers follow because they know that prices are on the rise, so asking for a low price ensures they will get the maximum number of purchase offers. As a result, a bidding war follows, and the price goes sky high. Therefore, if you are interested in buying an investment property in a seller's market, do not go below the asking price.

**2. How long property has been on the market versus the market value:** Now that you know the market conditions, check the time the property you are interested in has been up for sale (days on market). Such data is publicly available on the MLS and other sites about finding investment properties. This information will give you an insight into the overall state of an area's housing market. It is also a good indicator of buyers' interest to know whether the seller has priced the home fairly. As a real estate investor, your offer on a house has to reflect both the current local demand while being in line with other potential offers. For example, say the average home takes up to a month to go into contract in your housing market, but the property in question has been up for sale for longer than two months. This tells you that the seller has priced the home too high and is struggling to attract bids. In this case, the seller will be more likely to accept an offer lower than the list price. Plus, the longer a property has been on the market, the less of an upper hand the seller will have in negotiation. On the other hand, a seller who has just listed the property for sale will expect offers at or above the list price. As you can see, by paying attention to this property data, you can get a better idea of how much you should offer on a house.

**3. Competition for the property:** You might be up against not only regular homebuyers, but also other real estate investors like yourself with all-cash offers. Before sending your offer, ask your real estate agent to ask the seller's agent about recent showing activity. The seller's agent will probably not reveal whether there are other offers, but they may admit that there isn't much serious interest in the house or, conversely, that there has been a lot of recent interest. This type of information will help you determine your offer price. For example, if you know it's unlikely for the property to have much competition, you can make your offer lower than the list price, as you will likely have an opportunity to negotiate. On the other hand, if the seller has multiple offers on hand and you know there will be competition, your offer has to be more seller-friendly (i.e. higher offer price and fewer seller-paid costs). You might also want to put an *escalation clause* in your offer. This basically allows you to say, "I'll pay X price for this home, but if the seller gets a higher offer, I'm willing to increase my offer to Y price." Doing this not only makes negotiations easier, but you will stand out as a serious buyer and increase your chances of scoring a new real estate investment.

**4. Seller's motivations and needs:** Often, buyers go into writing an offer thinking it should only meet their needs. However, the strongest offers are those that address the needs of both the buyer and seller. In fact, the seller's motivations are just as important as the housing market's conditions; therefore, finding the middle ground will be where the best real estate deals lie. Smart real estate investors try to get as much information as possible about the seller from the listing agent to determine how much they should offer on a house around those needs. Conclusively, it is also likely that the seller will notice the effort, which will help in setting your offer apart from the crowd.

## TIPS ON MAKING YOUR OFFER STAND OUT AND ACCEPTED

There is serious competition in the real estate world, and as a result, properties are being sold out in a mere couple days. For this reason, it is important that you know how to write an offer letter that stands out, and you can do that with the following tips.

1. **Show you can buy the property:** One of the biggest fears a seller has is taking the property off the market for a month or more, only to find that the deal falls through when the buyer is unable to obtain financing. If you are a cash buyer, proving you can afford the property is easy. Simply submit a bank or brokerage account statement along with your offer showing that you have enough money to buy the property. However, if you are planning to finance the property, it is a good idea to submit a preapproval letter from a reputable lender. This shows that not only can you afford the property, but the lender has done the necessary credit, income, and asset verifications to ensure they are actually willing to give you a loan. Note that this is different from a pre-qualification—a preapproval is a commitment to loan you money, provided that the property meets the lender's standards and your situation does not change dramatically.

2. **Offer a large earnest deposit (standard is around 1 to 3% of price):** When you submit an offer to buy a property, it is standard practice to submit a small deposit to show the seller that you mean business. This is known as an *earnest deposit*, or *earnest money*. Essentially, if you fail to buy the property and do not have a contractually valid reason, the earnest deposit is given to the seller. Expectations for earnest deposits vary by market, but roughly 1% of the home's value is a good rule of thumb. For example, if you're offering $479,000 for a home, it is usually reasonable to offer a $5,000 earnest deposit. However, in some markets, a smaller deposit is standard ($500 to $1,000), regardless of the home's value, and in hotter markets, a higher amount could be expected. Here's one secret—if you want to make your offer

stand out, include a larger-than-expected earnest check. If $5,000 is expected, consider offering $10,000. After all, your earnest deposit is applied toward the purchase of the home when you get to the closing table, so it won't cost you any additional money in the end.

**3. Do not ask the seller to pay closing costs.**

**4. Demonstrate patience about taking possession.**

**5. Work with a real estate agent that can help you through the process.**

**6. Be prepared to walk away from a property.**

7. **Adjust contingencies:** There are three major contingencies that can appear in most real estate contracts, and by getting a little creative, you could use them to make your offer stand out.

- **Financing:** I never suggest waiving the financing contingency unless you are prepared to pay cash for the property, even if you are 99.99% sure that you can get approved for a loan.
- **Inspection:** It is generally not a good idea to waive your right to inspect, unless you are planning to renovate the property completely or tear it down. However, you could offer a shorter inspection period, say, five days from the contract date instead of 10.
- **Appraisal:** For most buyers, if you plan to waive one of your contingencies, this is it. Essentially, the appraisal contingency gives you a way out of the deal if the property does not appraise for the

contract price. By waiving this, you're agreeing to purchase the property, even if the appraisal comes in low. In hot real estate markets, this can be very appealing to a seller. The risk is that if the appraisal comes in too low, your lender might not want to loan you as much as you expect, and you will have to cover the difference out of pocket.

## HOW TO CONVINCE SOMEONE TO SELL THEIR PROPERTY TO YOU

Now that you know what to write in an offer letter to stand out from the rest, it is imperative that you know how to get the seller to accept your offer and give you their property. The tips I will show you will be helpful in what you should write in your offer letter.

1. **Focus on making a connection:** It is important to find a common interest between you and the seller because people tend to like others with similar interests. Tell the seller how much their home would mean to you; talk about the children you plan to play with in the backyard and salute their charitable efforts. In your letter, it is important to tell them who you are and why you are a good person. Selling a home is extremely emotional, especially if they have lived in it for many years. So, a seller would much rather sell to a family who works at a non-profit looking to eradicate poverty than to a 25-year-old trust fund kid whose parents are paying the entire down payment. This means you have to tell your story in a positive light by sharing the struggles you had to overcome. The purchaser of my home wrote a nice letter that told me how much he loved my house's brick facade and that it reminded him of the colonial homes in Virginia where he grew up and went to college. Given I, too, went to high school and college in Virginia, I was more willing to

entertain his offer, especially since he and his girlfriend had a two-year-old son. So, use your story to work your magic on the seller. You can find certain information about the seller on the internet or through your real estate agent.

**2. Allude to end-of-the-world scenarios:** It is much more stressful being a seller than a buyer. Buyers can simply shop around with no commitments. However, the seller is putting themselves out there by listing their property online, signing a contract with a real estate agent, and allowing strangers to go through their home. The seller also knows that if they do not sell within a certain period, the property goes "stale fish." It is embarrassing when you put yourself out there and get no sale. As a result of so much worry and stress, using *the end of the world* strategy can really motivate your seller to offload. You can start off with big picture scenarios, such as discussing what would happen to the property market if the stock market has a 50%+ correction like it did in 2008-2009. Then you can go on to discuss what would happen if there was a terrorist attack. Finally, you can talk about natural disasters like earthquakes, flooding, and fire potentially wiping away their property for good. Your goal is to make the seller believe their house is a riskier asset than it really is. When I was in the process of selling my rental property, I kept thinking about how lucky I was to have escaped a big earthquake during my 13 years of ownership in San Francisco. The house was in The Marina district, which has loose soil that is susceptible to liquefaction. The key is to ask about the potential risk of each scenario and not tell. Asking gets the seller thinking about worst case scenarios.

**3. Focus on the benefits of a simple life**: Life is much simpler renting and owning fewer things. Bad tenants, leaky roofs, endless maintenance, and ever-increasing property tax are terrible things. The older the property seller, the more appealing a simple life free from property maintenance will be. After a decade of homeownership, a property owner will have experienced more than their fair share of troubles. However, you can still argue about the joys of simpler living to younger property sellers too because they can definitely remember what it was like as a renter. Convincing the seller about the benefits of a simple life highlighting all the remodeling and upgrades you plan to do to the property. Not only do you make the seller feel good knowing you plan to take care of the house, but by discussing all the work you plan to do, you also remind the seller of how much work they have to do if they were to keep the property.

4. **Hone your persuasion skills:** Everybody has a motivation. If you can figure out what they are and make a connection, you can probably get at least a couple percentages off fair market value. An example would be if my San Francisco rental house buyer had made a connection with me over tennis or got me worried about an 8+ Richter scale earthquake hitting San Francisco in the next five years. In that case, I would have probably sold the house for $140,000 less (5%) than I did. Even 5% less was still 4% higher than the selling price I wanted.

Finally, if the seller has no competition, do not be afraid to offer less (lowball offer) than the asking price. However, do not merely state the price you are willing to pay, but use your negotiation skills to lower the price. Do not offer too little, as it might offend the seller, and they likely will not be willing to proceed with you. If you are not strong in negotiating, it is best to hire a real estate agent who is good at it.

## WHAT COMES NEXT AFTER A SELLER ACCEPTS YOUR OFFER

After a seller accepts your offer, visit the home many times before the closing day. This visit will include going there with your real estate agent, property inspectors, contractors, appraisers, etc. You should also make sure you schedule a final walkthrough, which your realtor will set up. Listed are the things you will need to do after your offer has been accepted and the property marked as contingent or pending.

1. The property will be marked as contingent or pending.

2. Contact your real estate agent, lender, inspector, insurance, and contractors (to get repair or maintenance estimates), inform them about the status of the property, and fix the inspection and closing dates.

3. Submit earnest and due diligence money to your real estate agent immediately, as failure to do so will cause a breach of contract. This due diligence money allows you to inspect a property once the seller has accepted your offer. Also, since your due diligence money is valid for an agreed timeframe between you and the seller, make sure your lender does their appraisal within this period. If there is a need for a time extension, then discuss such with the seller.

4. Send relevant documents to your lender (if any). Your lender will require items like W2's and other identifiable tax-related information, as they will need to verify your income. Once you can deliver these documents early enough, you will close on time on the property too. It will also be smart to connect your lender and realtor to each other on time, so they can help speed things up.

5. Set a closing date with your real estate attorney. You should make sure you schedule the closing early enough, so the attorney you want to work with has time on that day. Connect your real estate agent to your lender and attorney so they can work together because your attorney will need their forms filled out to prepare your closing.

6. Do house inspection, due diligence, and home appraisal. Having your home appraised is part of what ensures the money the bank is giving you is enough, meaning they can recoup most of it if you stop paying your mortgage. A home appraisal is the bank's way of figuring out if the amount of money they are lending to you is more or less than the value of your home, and that you are not over-paying for something. Many real estate agents will tell you there is no way you can overpay for a home because the bank appraises it. Although there is some truth to that, it is safe to say it still isn't 100% accurate. You have options when the home does not appraise with a chance to negotiate a better price. I have seen homes appraise for a lot less than they should and also those that appraise for more than their market value.

7. Make repairs and other requests based on findings from due diligence. Once you have gotten back reports from the inspectors, you will negotiate the repairs with the seller. Some sellers will be willing to make the repairs with you, whereas others will not oblige. More often than not, there will be a mutual resolution during these due diligence repair negotiations. Sometimes the seller will make the repairs or provide the buyer with a financial concession at closing, so they can make them with their own contractors. Ultimately, what matters most is that both the buyer and seller go home happy.

8. Get home insurance. Home insurance is an important step when buying a home. Make sure you find an insurance agent you like and that your insurance plan covers everything that you want it to. Plans are typically based on several factors, so be sure you check in with a few different home insurance agents. Many buyers choose the first one, only to realize later that they spent a couple hundred dollars more than they needed to, so always compare quotes whether it is a lender, realtor, attorney, contractor, inspector, etc.

## YOUR DUE DILIGENCE CHECKLIST

This property investment due diligence checklist comprises all the assets and liabilities of the property you are about to purchase. Using it as a guide, you can conduct detailed research on your desired property and weigh out the benefits before deciding. Often, offers will depend on what is found here.

1. **Financial confirmation:** This includes the total and current expenses and income statements, including the current rent roll and aged receivables report. Go back at least five years when looking for leasing costs and capital expenses to make sure the profit margin that the seller said the property has is accurate.

2. **Property physical confirmation:** Get a professional property inspector to help you check structure, electric fittings, HVAC, roofing, foundation, construction, insulation, etc. to make sure they are all in great shape or if they are needing minor repairs. This is because a property inspector will see flaws that would not otherwise be visible to you. Also, you can get the appraisal of the property

rechecked, so you can be sure everything is the way they say it is.

**3. Environmental and geotechnical reports:** This includes checking for any lead or asbestos, mold and mildew buildup, etc. Any of these substances found on the property will indicate a risk to the living environment in the long run. Also, the geotechnical aspects, such as soil reports and other land-related documents, are important in figuring out the durability of the property.

**4. Compliance with Americans with Disabilities Act (ADA Compliance):** The ADA requires that property owners incorporate certain utilities and amenities in the design and construction of the property to support disabled residents. Under the ADA, all housing properties must comply with these requirements and each property must have a certificate confirming compliance. You should check the certificate thoroughly, lest you run into legal trouble after acquiring the property. If there isn't any certificate verifying its compliance, you can get it investigated yourself to avoid further expenses and legal issues.

**5. Tenancy investigation:** The best way to go about this is to get your hands on a list of all previous tenants. The list should include everything from their rent amount, payments, tenancy period, and lease details. Additionally, you should get all the details on other cost pools, like overcharge and late rent fees to the tenants. Other important aspects to check during tenancy due diligence include the amendments and subleases added to tenant leases, if any. This will help you find any long-standing tenant issues and resolve them before you acquire the property. After that, send these lease details for verification because it will help you create a good relationship with the tenants and ensure a smooth transition of ownership.

6. **Taxation review:** It is crucial that you get a thorough taxation review of your property, so none of the amount ends up on your end after the deal is closed. You can quickly get this information from your appraiser or neighborhood tax collector. Reviewing the real estate tax bills will give you an idea of the amount you will have to pay as tax in the future. That is why checking previous bills can help you decide whether the property is profitable for you. You can also get your own tax bill estimate from the tax collector to know the amount for sure.

7. **Contracts and insurance:** Conducting proper due diligence on all contracts and insurance policies can help you avoid legal issues. So, look for any pending litigation regarding the property from the past and get an insurance quotation yourself and compare it to the current insurance policy. This can help you get a clear representation of the insurance and its effect on the property.

In conclusion, you can negotiate the price and other terms if you find some problems during due diligence. Also, be willing to walk away from a property if there are any deal breakers.

## CHAPTER SUMMARY

- For a real estate investor, putting together a strong purchase offer is the single most important step to buying an investment property. It is what determines whether you will become the new property owner or start your property search all over again.

- As a general rule in real estate investing, the less money you pay up front, the higher the ROI. However, if you offer it at a cheap price, you risk having the seller write you off completely. So, how can you make sure your offer will be the one the seller cannot refuse? The answer to this is striking the right balance where both you (the investor) and the seller get what you want.
- After a seller accepts your offer, visit the home many times before the closing day. This visit will include going there with your real estate agent, property inspectors, contractors, appraisers, etc.

In the next chapter, you will learn how to rent out your property.

# CHAPTER SIX: RENTING YOUR PROPERTY

There are a couple factors that an investor can put in place to boost their property's appeal and potential for attracting quality tenants. Not only does an appealing rental property have a higher chance of getting a high-quality tenant, but the chances are that they will take better care of it. Therefore, before you open the doors to property hunters, ensure your rental property investment has a winning edge over its competitors with the following tips.

## HOW TO PREPARE YOUR PROPERTY FOR RENTAL

1. It does not have to look as great as a house you are trying to sell.
2. It is okay to go with linoleum counters instead of granite, white appliances instead of stainless steel, and painted cabinets instead of brand new ones.
3. The rehabilitation and repairs you have estimated

for during due diligence and inspection should already have been done.

4. Check current regulations or safety guidelines to make sure the property meets them.
5. Make sure it has the basic requirements (working appliances, phone/internet, heating and cooling, curtains/blinds, good water pressure, and smoke detectors).
6. Organize services and utilities.
7. Fix anything that is broken.
8. Clean and deodorize—surpass the standard cleaning and invest in professional cleaning.
9. Search for and eradicate mold.
10. Rekey or change locks—change locks between tenants (i.e. before a new tenant moves into your property, change the locks that the previous tenant had access to).
11. Paint the walls.
12. Spruce up the landscaping.
13. Clean or replace curtains and window screens and wash windows.
14. Service central air system.
15. Restore hardwood floors.
16. Style it up to stand out.

## REASONS FOR HIRING A PROPERTY MANAGER

One major decision you will make as an investor/landlord is deciding if you should hire a property management company. Many landlords manage their properties on their own or with the help of a resident manager. But sometimes, landlords need more help, and that is when a property management company might be a good investment. Although property management companies will be a huge asset to your business, they are expensive. Management companies also help you handle prospects and tenants, thus saving you time and worry over marketing your rentals, collecting rent, handling maintenance and repair issues, responding to tenant complaints, and even pursuing evictions.

More importantly, a good management company will bring its expertise and experience to your property, giving you the assurance that comes with knowing your investment is in good hands. Finally, a management company is also an independent contractor, so you can avoid the hassles of being an employer. However, hiring a property manager is not everyone's forte, so the following factors may indicate that it is a good idea to hire a property management company for your business.

1. When you do not live near your rental property.
2. When your time is limited.
3. When you have a lot of rental properties.
4. When you are not interested in hands-on management.
5. When you do not know anything about managing property.
6. When you can afford the cost.
7. When your property is part of an affordable housing program.
8. When you are willing to give up control.
9. When you have a high vacancy rate or problems with cash flow.
10. When you do not want to deal with tenants or evictions.

## HOW TO FIND A GOOD PROPERTY MANAGER

You can never be too careful when scouting for a property manager/management company to hire. It will only be wise for you to do your findings so you do not end up with regrets. The following tips will get you started in hiring a property manager that suits your needs.

1. Get recommendations from colleagues or your agent.
2. Search professional directories.
3. Interview companies.
4. Ask about their fees, including for additional services.
5. Ask about where they will place funds, collections, etc.
6. Ask about how they maintain property.

## DUTIES OF A PROPERTY MANAGER

The following are the duties of a property management company:

1. Setting rent.
2. Collecting rent.
3. Screening tenants.
4. Property maintenance.
5. Managing budgets.

## HOW TO FIND GOOD TENANTS

Finding quality tenants is just as important as preparing your property for rent. Having the wrong tenants is one of the worst things that could happen to an investor because not only will it likely cause you lack of sleep, but it will also cost you time and money.

To find high-quality tenants, the first thing you need to do before you begin is to familiarize yourself with fair housing laws. These differ from state-to-state.

**1. Use a waiting list of tenants:** Most successful landlords keep an active waiting list for their properties. When somebody asks whether you have any rental property available, and you do not, you can respond by saying, *"I do not right now, but I might have something soon. May I have your name, phone number, and email?"* Add their contact information in a note labeled *"waiting list tenants,"* and follow them up when you have a vacant property. Most landlords will not follow up, and even if the prospective tenant does not rent your property, you might have still made a new connection for the future.

**2. Use social media and your connections:** Talk about your vacant rental properties on social media, show pictures and videos of your property talking about the quality of the house and its affordability. Tell your social media connections to share the videos and pictures with their friends just in case someone might need a space. Your friends might know good tenants they can recommend to you. To make it a sweeter deal, you could add an incentive like a referral bonus whenever their referrals actually rent your property. Do this and see how many recommendations you get.

**3. Source from non-profit and medical organizations, as well as from companies:** Most landlords do not use this resource. However, there are some landlords who use only this resource. There are several nonprofits that rent housing for their organization. For example, assume you are building a 100-unit apartment complex across the street from a hospital. You can get the hospital or a company to pre-lease, maybe 40 units for staff housing. Or you could also reserve a unit for a nonprofit that works with refugees. This is a good strategy to rent out to tenants in bulk while also earning in bulk.

**4. Follow the law:** Do not discriminate by race, nationality, religion, familial status, or disability (Federal Fair Housing Act).

**5. Choose a tenant with:**

- Good credit (verify income, run a credit check, criminal check).
- Good rental history (check with previous landlords).
- Stable employment.
- Maximum of two people per bedroom.

## PREPARING FOR A NEW TENANT

A new tenant moving into your rental property can be stressful for both the tenant and you, the landlord. Nevertheless, having a checklist of items that must be looked into before the tenant moves in will help make the transition easier and ensure you do not miss any important steps. Below are ten things you should address before having a new tenant move into your rental property.

1. Review and sign the lease with the tenant.
2. Collect the first month's rent and security deposit.

3. Have the necessary property inspections completed.
4. Go through the move-in checklist.
5. Provide the tenant with your/the property manager's contact information.
6. Go through any specific tenant requests or conditions.

In situations whereby the tenant wants more than the necessities you have provided, you can decide if you want to honor such requests. If you would, then make sure to add their special requests as a clause in your lease agreement. For example, if you are going to charge the tenant $400 to paint the apartment, you will need to include that in your lease so you can have written proof that the tenant has agreed to the terms.

## NEW TENANT CHECKLIST

A new tenant checklist is a series of bullet points itemizing tasks and issues that must be completed and addressed before the tenant can take possession of the rental property. For example, you will have to find new tenants for all the available rental units when you buy a new rental property. Now, if a tenant's lease is about to expire, and they have been given notice that they would terminate the rental agreement, you will have to find a new tenant to fill that vacancy. You will also have to search for a new tenant if you must evict someone because they violated the terms of the lease agreement. You must take legal steps to carry out the eviction.

A general checklist can be broken down into five basic categories:

1. **Steps 1-8:** Tenant screening.

2. **Steps 9-16:** Lease procedures.
3. **Steps 17- 19:** Financial considerations.
4. **Steps 20- 24:** Preparing the property.
5. **If Applicable:** Any extra requirements in your lease or for a specific tenant.

Below is a sample of a new tenant checklist. Please note that your checklist will depend on your procedures for screening tenants, how in-depth your lease agreement is, and the steps involved in having them move in. You can and should create a list that's unique to your rental property.

Sample New Tenant Checklist

**Tenant(s) Name(s):**______________________________

**Property Address:**______________________________

**Unit Number:**______________________________

**Move-In Date:**______________________________

1._____ Received Rental Application

2._____ Started a New Physical Folder for Tenant

3._____ Started a New Digital Folder for Tenant

4._____ Background Check Completed

5._____ Credit Check Completed

6._____ Received Employment Verification Form

7._____ Received Previous Landlord Verification Form

8._____ Made Copies of Back and Front of Tenant(s) ID(s)

9._____ Explained All Rules and Procedures to Tenant

10._____ Explained Emergency Procedures to Tenant

11._____ Tenant Signed Lease Agreement

12._____ Tenant Signed Lease Agreement Addendums

______________________________Which Ones?

13._____ Date Lease Agreement Signed

14._____ Date Lease Begins

15._____ Date Lease Ends

16.______ Provided Tenant With Your Contact Information

17._____ Received Entire Security Deposit via Certified Method

___________Date Security Deposit Received

18._____ Received Entire First Month's Rent via Certified Method

___________Date First Month's Rent Received

19. _____Tenant Has Purchased Renter's Insurance

20._____ Repaired Any Damage to Property

21._____ Cleaned Property

22._____ Tenant has Signed Rental Unit Condition Checklist

23._____ Changed Door Locks (If Applicable)

24._____ Transferred All Utilities to Tenant's Name (if applicable)

Utility:_________ Date of Transfer:______________

Utility:_________ Date of Transfer:______________

Utility:_________ Date of Transfer:______________

**If Applicable**

1._________ Property Inspected for Certificate of Habitability

_________Date of Inspection

2._________ Received Deposit to Hold Agreement and Necessary Funds

3. _________ Pet Addendum Signed

4._________ Pet Deposit Received

5._________ Lead Disclosure Warning Signed (For Property Built Before 1978)

---

6._________ Gave Tenant "Protect Your Family from Lead Paint" Pamphlet

7._________ Section 8 Paperwork Received

__________Spoke With Section 8 Case Worker

____Y/N__ Section 8 Inspection Occurred _________Date of Inspection

___________Security Deposit Received From Section 8 Tenant

**Date All Items Completed:______________________________**

**Signature of Landlord/Property Manager:_________________________**

Finally, make your own checklist into summary form with highlights that your tenant will need as they settle in. And for your own sake, take a final picture of the property before you turn it over to your tenant, so you can have proof of the condition in which you delivered it, just in case there is any disagreement.

## CONSIDERATIONS FOR YOUR LEASE

A lease is the binding agreement between the tenant and landlord that outlines the responsibilities of each party. This often includes:

1. Rules on pets.
2. Rules on altering property, painting.
3. Instructions for parking vehicles.
4. Process for requesting repairs.
5. Rent due dates and late fees.
6. How to remit payment.
7. Lease rate escalation on renewal.

Leases can be two or 20 pages long. Although there are dozens of free leases that can be downloaded online, it is best to have a real estate attorney review or prepare the agreement for you.

## MAINTENANCE

There are two options regarding managing and maintaining a property: do it yourself or hire someone to do the job for you. Maintaining the property includes the following:

1. Monthly extermination.
2. Checking for water damage or leaks after a heavy

rainstorm, after snow begins to melt, or on hot and humid days.

3. Examining shower caulking and grout between tiles.
4. Testing the smoke and carbon monoxide detectors regularly.
5. Changing filters in forced air systems.
6. Flushing the water heater.
7. Clean the gutters.
8. Understanding the legal regulations on maintenance and repairs.
9. Between tenants, bringing the property back to rental condition.

Quality maintenance may increase your short-term costs, but keeping the property in the best condition will preserve its value in the long run. In addition, refurbishing your rental property before putting it on the market will make it more attractive to prospective tenants. This ultimately lowers your vacancy expenses and motivates future tenants to take care of the property after signing the lease.

## FINANCIAL CONTINGENCIES

In a home sale and purchase agreement, financing contingency refers to a clause that expresses the offer as contingent on the buyer, securing financing for the property. A financing contingency provides the buyer with protection from potential legal consequences in case the deal fails to close. Below are some financial contingencies you can rely on to secure the financing for your property.

## CONTINGENCY FUNDS

This is the cash for holding costs to cover mortgage, insurance, and taxes for one to two months while fixing up the property and finding a tenant. It is a large reserve fund to cover *"known unknowns"* (which are things that are known to happen, but you cannot tell when they will happen). Examples include vacancies, roof repairs, tree maintenance, etc. They are the reserve fund to cover two months of expenses for every property, and you are to commit to replenishing when you draw from it.

## HAVE A SECURED LINE OF CREDIT FOUR EACH PROPERTY BASED ON THE EQUITY YOU HAVE BUILT UP.

A line of credit is a flexible loan from a financial institution that consists of a defined amount of money, which an investor can have access to as needed and repay either immediately or over time. Interest is charged on a line of credit as soon as money is borrowed. This provides security and access to fast cash for unexpected, enormous expenses *(unknown unknowns).*

## LANDLORD INSURANCE

Landlord insurance covers property damage, lost rental income, and liability protection in case a tenant or visitor suffers injury as a result of property maintenance issues. Thus, in addition to homeowners' insurance, try to get some landlord insurance.

## HOW TO INCREASE YOUR RENTAL INCOME

Before you think of or start raising your rent, you should do some market research and find out the current rate for rent in your neighborhood. The reason is pretty clear—raising the rent too high will certainly generate complaints from tenants and could even lead to you losing a good tenant leaving to find something more affordable. So, check the market rate for rent in the area of your property by talking to property managers who handle similar properties or real estate agents and looking at rental advertisements.

After checking out the current market rent, and if you believe it is not a bad idea to raise the rent, you will need to send a letter to inform your tenants, 30 or 60 days before, that you will be doing so. Below are strategic ways you can raise rent.

1. Rent out parking spots.
2. Rent out storage space.
3. Charge for laundry.
4. Add a secondary dwelling suite.
5. Turn some units into short term furnished rentals.
6. Renovate and improve your property (list down what renovations add value and what does not).

Let's see a sample of a rent increment notice I drafted for one of my rental properties.

**Notice of Rent Increase for Month to Month Tenants**

Name of Tenant
Address of Tenant
Unit Number

This Notice is to inform you that beginning on, ***Insert Date of Rent Increase***, the monthly rent for the unit you currently occupy, Unit ***Insert Unit Number***, which is located at, ***Insert Property Address***, will be increased to ***Insert New Monthly Rent*** per month. This rental payment is due on or before the 5th day of each month.

If you wish to continue your tenancy, the new monthly rental payment of ***Insert New Monthly Rent*** is required. Please be advised that all other terms of your original rental agreement remain in effect.

Please sign the Notice below, indicating your agreement and continued tenancy or indicating your disagreement and subsequent termination of tenancy.

Thank you. We appreciate your continued tenancy.

Sincerely,

**Landlord's Signature:**____________________________ **Date:**________________________

____________________

___I agree to the new monthly rent amount of *Insert New Monthly Rent* beginning on *Insert Date of Rent Increase* and will continue my month to month tenancy as per our original rental agreement.

**Tenant**
**Signature:**_______________________ **Date:**_______________
_______________

___I do not agree to the new monthly rent of *Insert New Monthly Rent*. I will not continue my month to month tenancy and will vacate the premises by *Insert Move-Out Date* according to the terms of our original rental agreement.

**Tenant**
**Signature:**_______________________ **Date:**_______________
_______________________

## LEGAL OBLIGATIONS INVESTORS (YOU) SHOULD KNOW ABOUT

1. Landlord-tenant laws in state and locale.
2. **Tenants' rights:** Federal law prohibits discrimination of tenants on the basis of *race, color, religion, national origin, sex, age, familial status (including not allowing children and discrimination against pregnant women), physical disability,* and *mental disability (including alcoholism and past drug addiction).*
3. Obligations on security deposits, lease requirements, eviction rules, and fair housing.
4. Do not wait too long before beginning the eviction process. Follow through with your lease agreement.

## RENTAL PROPERTY ACCOUNTING

As a real estate investor—especially a busy one managing a portfolio of rental properties—it might be tempting to let administrative work like bookkeeping take the back burner because of the work involved with filing receipts or reconciling expenses. However, if you set up an effective rental property accounting system, it will help you run your real estate business smoothly, make sure you get the most out of your investments, and give you time to focus on profit-making activities. Rental property accounting involves bookkeeping, which involves recording financial transactions for individuals or businesses.

As an investor managing a portfolio of rental properties, there are certain questions you should have answers to, such as: *how will I manage the constant flow of rent checks, management fees, and maintenance invoices? How do I know which of my properties are eating into my profits?* Staying on top of your bookkeeping is the solution to safeguarding your business and maximizing your financial performance.

Below are the steps for setting up a solid bookkeeping system for your rental properties.

1. **Get a tax professional and bookkeeper:** Rental property accounting, when done correctly, brings the following advantages to you as a real estate investor: safeguarding your business against debt or fraud, forecasting future expenses, and saving time and resources during tax season. Also, if you are an investor with an LLC, you may enjoy additional accounting principles and tips. But I recommend that you consult a financial professional to help you implement financial tracking for your business. And remember—accounting is just one example of the many real estate systems out there that can help you maximize your

efficiency and minimize your errors, so you can channel your energy into activities that will boost your income.

**2. Separate business and personal accounts:** You would be setting up your rental property business for failure if you keep the money from your personal and business transactions together. Open financial accounts for your business, such as checking and savings accounts, credit cards, and debit cards. This separation ensures that all the income and expenses flowing in and out of your business does not get mixed up with your personal affairs.

**3. Set up individual accounts for each property:** As your rental property business grows, ensure that you open separate accounts for each rental property that you own. By doing so, your income and expenses will be kept separate on a per-property basis. It will make things easier for you regarding reconciling, preparing profit and loss statements, and filing taxes. In addition, keeping your financial data unique to each property will allow you to identify any particular properties or units that are eating into your rental income.

**4. Have a system to track your income and expenses:** Once you have set up separate accounts for each of your properties, you will need a reliable system for tracking the inflows and outflows of cash for your properties and your business overall. Some investors might design their own expense worksheets, whereas others may opt to use a rental property accounting software to keep track of their finances.

**5. Choose between cash or accrual accounting:** If you prefer to record income and expenses as they occur, regardless of when the cash is received or paid, you should use the accrual method. On the other hand, you can use the cash method if you prefer to log income and expenses as they hit your account. Deciding which method to choose will be dependent on your personal preference and what works best for your business. However the most important thing is staying consistent and sticking to one accounting method when recording your transactions.

**6. Take advantage of accounting technology:** I highly recommend that investors go digital for all things accounting and bookkeeping. This includes the use of scanning applications to digitize receipts and invoices or investing in accounting software to integrate your bookkeeping, file storage, and financial analysis in one place. Digitization will help you declutter your office, stay on top of your invoicing, and even contribute to saving the planet. Also, if you would like to share data with professionals across your team, cloud-based software may be your best option.

## CHAPTER SUMMARY

- One major decision you will make as an investor/landlord is deciding if you should hire a property management company. Many landlords manage their properties on their own or with the help of a resident manager. However, sometimes landlords need more help, and that is when a property management company might be a good investment.
- Landlord insurance is a type of insurance that covers property damage, lost rental income, and liability protection in case a tenant or visitor

suffers injury as a result of property maintenance issues.

- Having a checklist of items that must be looked into before the tenant moves in will help make the transition easier and ensure you do not miss any important steps.

In the next chapter, you will learn how to add to your rental property.

# CHAPTER SEVEN: ADDING TO YOUR RENTAL PROPERTY

Since you now know how to rent your investment property and earn from it, the next thing for you to know is how you can add more to the rental property that you already have, so you can have even more cash flow. In owning more rental properties as a real estate investment, you will need to learn how to manage your portfolio of rental properties, which many real estate investors do not know how to do, and that is why they either fail at expansion or just stay in their comfort zone of owning only one property.

In this chapter, I will show you how you can add to your rental property portfolio regularly until you reach the desired monthly cash flow you need for an early retirement. Because it is easier to reach early retirement through multiple rental properties than from having just one. Keep in mind the amount you will need to have for investment and the number of rental properties to invest in, as well as the target rate of return *(refer to chapter two).*

1. The first thing you will want to ask yourself when wondering how to buy multiple properties is if that property will give you a high return on investment and cash-on-cash return. When most people buy a property, they make the mistake of mixing up their emotions with the purchase. They love how the investment property looks and feels and tend to overpay. By keeping a level head and always doing a comparative market analysis, you can avoid making mistakes and continue to buy multiple properties below market value, or at least properties with a solid future growth potential. The last thing you want is to buy a property that looks nice, only to find out that you are losing your money.

2. Buy your first property below the market value, which could be a foreclosed home or those that have been on the market for too long *(refer to chapter two for more details).*

3. Property investors who are experts on buying multiple properties always recommend that you find a good mortgage broker. The reason is that financing investment property is much harder than it was before. That is why having a great mortgage broker by your side can help increase your borrowing capacity and get you approved for more mortgage loans. By receiving more loans, you can grow your real estate investment portfolio faster.

4. Add value to your property through renovation/repairs. Properties that are in poor condition and need repairs are often bought well below market value compared to similar, well-kept properties because not everyone wants to put work into them. Smart real estate investors will add a great deal of equity to their investment property quickly by making renovations that are not so expensive.

5. Speed up your property growth by leveraging the equity you have in your properties. In doing this, you have two options: **option one** is to sell the property and get cash left over and **option two** is to borrow money (up to 80% of the equity) against the equity. For example, if you buy a property for $300,000 and assume it goes up in value to $400,000, then you will have $100,000 in equity in this property.

6. Get your property values reviewed constantly because knowing whether your property has a higher valuation than before can help you if you want to know how to buy multiple properties. Higher valuation means that you can then have access to more equity for investing. It is true that property valuations cost money, but they are often tax deductible. It will be a smart move to get your investment property revalued if the current housing market is booming.

7. Make sure each property you own has a positive cash flow (the net profit from a rental property), so each month, you would get a payment above all the expenses that were used to reinvest. The simple fact is that if you purchase and continue to purchase positive cash flow property, you can then service your loans and afford more property. This is because, with every property you buy, you are increasing your disposable income by increasing your passive income.

8. If you want to be a multi-property investor, then you will need to have a way of scanning the market quickly for good deals; basically, you will need an easy way to find the diamonds in the rough that will make you a fortune. To avoid investing in the wrong location, you will need to conduct a real estate market analysis and investment property analysis. *Real Estate Investar* is a great tool that can help you scan properties on the market quickly and find

properties that suit your investment criteria. Also, stay updated with the trends in your area. The real estate market is constantly changing, and governments are always updating laws and regulations concerning real estate. If you do not stay up-to-date, this can have huge implications on your property investments. For example, if you own a property in a mining town, and the government does a huge land release in the area, it can affect the supply and demand of real estate and could cause the value of your property to decline.

9. Keep an eye on your portfolio so you know which properties are performing well and which can be improved or should be sold out. Keep accurate finances of the incomings and outgoings of your property. Keep your eye on the condition of your property and speak to real estate agents about what you could do to increase the rental income or value. Also, choose your tenants wisely and make sure they pay on time and take care of your property. Pay just as close attention to your rental manager. If they are horrible, then you should invest in a new manager.

10. There is a saying that goes, "*You do not make money until you sell.*" Many investors keep their properties, even when the value drops because they are afraid of losing money. They may go as far as keeping the property for 10 years before it returns to the value they bought it for, and they proclaim to the world that they *haven't lost money.* But in the actual sense, they have lost money because you lose money when you keep a bad investment. Finance savvy people call this *opportunity loss.*

11. Do not cross-collateralize. Cross-collateralization refers to having multiple properties securing one loan. If

something bad happens, then the bank may force you to sell multiple properties to service one loan. You can avoid this by financing each property with a different lender. But it is best to speak to an accountant to discuss the finer points of avoiding cross-collateralisation.

12. An interest-only mortgage is a great way to lower your weekly/monthly expenses and save up cash flow for servicing more loans and purchasing multiple properties. Principal and interest loans have larger monthly expenses, meaning that you will have to find a way to pay for these loans, even if it means taking money out of your own pocket. These extra costs will limit how quickly you can save up money for future investments. By using interest-only loans, you give yourself the best chance of expanding into new properties due to the lower ongoing mortgage costs.

13. Not every property is a good investment; likewise, not every property is a good investment for you. What may be a good investment for me might be a terrible investment for you. However, many investors just go out and buy property without a second thought to their long-term investment plan. They just hope to make money. This can work for one or two properties, but if you want to buy more property than the average investor, then you will really need to have a strategy on how you will make money and what your end goal is. For instance, if your end goal is $70,000 in passive income in 10 years, then you will invest differently than someone whose end goal is $1,000,000 in equity in 15 years. Knowing your investment strategy will allow you to create a list of what you want in a property. With this, you can narrow your market down to just the properties that suit you and your strategy. The benefit of this is that you will

spend less time, make more money, and grow your portfolio quicker.

## LEVERAGED STRATEGY (BUY AND HOLD MANY PROPERTIES) AND FREE AND CLEAR STRATEGY FOR RENTAL PROPERTY PORTFOLIO EXPANSION

In chapter two, I talked extensively on using the buy and hold strategy, its advantages compared to other forms of real estate investment strategies, and its disadvantages. I also talked extensively on the leveraged and free and clear strategies in real estate investment for early retirement. Furthermore, there are also sample computations, which can aid your understanding of the concepts.

So without any delay, let us study some real life scenarios (using you as the case study) with an average cash flow of $200 net as a starting point, rent increases of 3.3% per year, 4-unit properties, and the acquisition of a new property every three years using the ***leveraged strategy.***

1. **Average cash flow of $200:** Let us assume you are buying properties with an average cash flow of $200 per unit per month. If you buy in an above-average area or find an above-average deal (which is not hard to do if you take a few years to pick and choose), then you would speed up this timeline.

2. **Rent increases of 3.3%:** Assume the rent increases by 3.3% per year, based on historical averages.

3. **4-unit properties:** We will assume you are buying four-unit properties because they are the biggest ones you can acquire with residential loans (much more favorable) compared to commercial loans.

**4. New property every three years:** If you will buy one new property every three years, you could buy more if you have more capital available. Or, as your equity is paid down in Property #1, you could borrow a home equity line of credit against it for the down payment funds needed to buy another property.

NB: $200 per unit per month cash flow is just *today's numbers*. In three years, you should increase your standards as the market rent increases. So, by the time you buy Property #2, it should generate a minimum of $218/month cash flow per unit, or $874.18 for a fourplex.

| Year | Property 1 | Property 2 | Property 3 | Property 4 | Property 5 | Property 6 | TOTAL |
|---|---|---|---|---|---|---|---|
| 1 | $800.00 | | | | | | $800.00 |
| 2 | $826.40 | | | | | | $826.40 |
| 3 | $853.67 | | | | | | $853.67 |
| 4 | $881.84 | $874.18 | | | | | $1,756.02 |
| 5 | $910.94 | $903.03 | | | | | $1,813.97 |
| 6 | $941.00 | $932.83 | | | | | $1,873.83 |
| 7 | $972.06 | $963.61 | $955.24 | | | | $2,890.91 |
| 8 | $1,004.14 | $995.41 | $986.76 | | | | $2,986.31 |
| 9 | $1,037.27 | $1,028.26 | $1,019.33 | | | | $3,084.86 |
| 10 | $1,071.50 | $1,062.19 | $1,052.96 | $1,043.82 | | | $4,230.48 |
| 11 | $1,106.86 | $1,097.24 | $1,087.71 | $1,078.27 | | | $4,370.08 |
| 12 | $1,143.39 | $1,133.45 | $1,123.61 | $1,113.85 | | | $4,514.30 |
| 13 | $1,181.12 | $1,170.86 | $1,160.69 | $1,150.61 | $1,140.82 | | $5,804.09 |
| 14 | $1,220.10 | $1,209.50 | $1,198.99 | $1,188.58 | $1,178.47 | | $5,995.62 |
| 15 | $1,260.36 | $1,249.41 | $1,238.55 | $1,227.80 | $1,217.36 | | $6,193.48 |
| 16 | $1,301.95 | $1,290.64 | $1,279.43 | $1,268.32 | $1,257.53 | $1,246.38 | $7,644.24 |
| 17 | $1,344.92 | $1,333.23 | $1,321.65 | $1,310.17 | $1,299.03 | $1,287.51 | $7,896.50 |
| 18 | $1,389.30 | $1,377.23 | $1,365.26 | $1,353.41 | $1,341.90 | $1,330.00 | $8,157.09 |
| 19 | $1,435.14 | $1,422.67 | $1,410.32 | $1,398.07 | $1,386.18 | $1,373.89 | $8,426.27 |
| 20 | $1,482.50 | $1,469.62 | $1,456.86 | $1,444.20 | $1,431.92 | $1,419.23 | $8,704.34 |
| 21 | $1,531.43 | $1,518.12 | $1,504.93 | $1,491.86 | $1,479.18 | $1,466.06 | $8,991.58 |
| 22 | $1,581.96 | $1,568.22 | $1,554.60 | $1,541.10 | $1,527.99 | $1,514.44 | $9,288.30 |
| 23 | $1,634.17 | $1,619.97 | $1,605.90 | $1,591.95 | $1,578.41 | $1,564.42 | $9,594.82 |
| 24 | $1,688.10 | $1,673.43 | $1,658.89 | $1,644.49 | $1,630.50 | $1,616.04 | $9,911.45 |
| 25 | $1,743.80 | $1,728.65 | $1,713.63 | $1,698.75 | $1,684.31 | $1,669.37 | **$10,238.52** |

The above analysis shows 25 years of real estate investing.

Using this strategy, you could create a $5,000 per month of passive income in 12-13 years, or a $10,000 per month retirement in 25.

Let's see how you can expand your real estate portfolio using the ***free and clear strategy.***

The free and clear goal is to eventually own a relatively small, easy-to-manage number of residential real estate properties, free and clear of all debt. Although the plan can work with apartments, mobile homes, or commercial real estate, I would argue that in most cases, houses will be your best investments.

The end result could look like this:

10 single family houses owned free and clear.

$1,200 = Rent per month for each house.

($600) = Expenses per month for each house.

$600 = Net operating income per month for each house.

- $600 x 10 houses = $6,000 per month passive income.
- $6,000 x 12 = $72,000 per year passive income.

Would $72,000 per year coming in passively, consistently, and year after year change your life? Even if $72,000 per year does not work for you, just add a few more houses until you hit your number. Either way, I think you would agree that the end result is worthwhile. In summary, you should buy a property every few years. After at least 10 years of principal reduction and appreciation, sell Property #1 and use the proceeds to pay down the mortgages of their remaining portfolios. Reinvesting extra cash flow from yearly rent increases into paying down the principal balance. This can shorten your mortgage from 30 years to 17 years.

## TIPS FOR YOUR PROPERTY PORTFOLIO

1. **Focus on getting really good at a certain type of property investment rather than trying to invest in everything:** Find that one investment strategy that suits you, then study it intensively. Read books about it, attend seminars, and get your hands dirty by investing and testing out your strategy. Keep learning and getting better.

2. **Diversify your investments in different locations:** By spreading your investments across a variety of areas, you are increasing your chances of obtaining capital and rental growth each year. It is common for an area to go through a year where rent and house prices stay the same; however, it is very rare to find that across a number of areas or suburbs. Also, if one of your suburbs has a bad year, then you can still achieve growth on your other properties.

3. **Continue to get educated:** *"The best return on investment you will ever get is when you invest in your education."* The more you know about investing, the less money you need to make a lot of money; and the less you know, the more money you will need to make money. If you invest in your education, then the amount of money you can make from your investments becomes almost unlimited. However, if you do not educate yourself, it will be a long and tiring road toward financial freedom, and you will find that by the time you achieve that goal, you will already be too old to enjoy it.

## EXIT STRATEGIES

Exit strategies provide a plan of action and minimize forthcoming risks by helping an investor to remove themselves from a real estate investment deal. It is beneficial to investors who want to expand their real estate investment portfolio if one of them is not giving returns in terms of rental income. Thus, it is necessary for investors to evaluate potential exit strategies before purchasing investment properties.

**1. Wholesale:** This is putting a property under contract then assigning that contract to another real estate investor at a higher price. Let's assume you get a property under contract for $50,000 that will be worth $100,000 after completing $20,000 in renovations. You could wholesale this property to another investor for $60,000, and they would still have room to make a profit after they fix it up!

**2. Sale:** You need to understand that if you list the home with a realtor, you will traditionally pay out a 6% commission that would be split between the buyers' and sellers' agent(s). You may also be responsible for some of the closing costs and even repairs, depending on the results of the inspection. Be sure to factor this in before listing the home. Ensure you won't have to bring money to the closing table because you're losing money by selling the home. Also, selling your home as a ***for sale by owner*** (FSBO) might mean you're eliminating the realtor's commission, but FSBO homes stay on the market longer and sell for less money than homes sold by agents. Don't get sucked into the FSBO trap—just list the home with a realtor and avoid all the headaches of trying to do it yourself.

**3. Rent to Own:** This is when an investor rents their home to a tenant with the option for them to buy it.

**4. 1031 Exchange:** This means to defer paying capital gains by buying a similar property within a certain period with the profit gained from the sale of the first property.

**5. Refinancing:** In this case, the seller finances the real estate investing deal and acts as a bank. Then, the seller and buyer would exchange a promissory note, including an interest rate and repayment schedule. This exit strategy benefits sellers, as they are awarded monthly payments to cover the mortgage loan, and their return on investment increases through interest income.

## HOW TO CHOOSE THE BEST EXIT STRATEGY

Deciding on an exit strategy will require the following considerations:

1. Short and long-term goals.
2. Experience level.
3. Time to close.
4. Purchase price.
5. Property value.
6. Condition of the property.
7. Market conditions.
8. Supply and demand.
9. Financing options.
10. Profit potential.

## FACTORS THAT CAN RUIN AN EXIT STRATEGY

1. Depreciation.
2. Tenant issues resulting in lost rent.
3. Unexpected maintenance costs can cancel out profits.

4. Poor property management that reduces the value and potential cash flow.
5. A distinct lack of demand, failed escrow, or the backing out of a lender that may prevent the investment property from being flipped.

With all the information in this chapter, I'm confident in your abilities to add to your rental property portfolio regularly until you reach the desired monthly cash flow you need for retirement. Put this knowledge to work and be on your way to an early retirement.

## CHAPTER SUMMARY

In this chapter, you learned:

- How to add to your rental property portfolio regularly until you reach the desired monthly cash flow you need for early retirement.
- How to use the leveraged and free clear strategies for real estate investment.
- Tips for your property portfolio.
- How to choose the best exit strategy to minimize forthcoming risk.

# CONCLUSION

If you are working toward an early retirement, or you are simply looking for a step-by-step process into real estate investment, then I am sure *Building a Successful Retirement Plan Using Real Estate* has been super helpful to you. Every chapter contained strategic and actionable steps, including real-life scenarios, to help you start your journey into real estate investment.

In this book, I wrote extensively on the following helpful topics:

1. How to calculate the monthly rental income to aim for and figure out how much you need to save up to invest in real estate.
2. How to start investing in rental properties.
3. How you can afford to invest in real estate rental properties, even if you do not have a lot of money.
4. How to decide on what to invest in based on several evaluation methods.
5. How you can get your offer noticed and chosen amongst others.

6. The steps needed to have your property rented out and earn money for you.
7. How you can add to your rental property portfolio regularly until you reach the desired monthly cash flow you need for retirement.

With all the tools (information) you have gleaned in this book, you can confidently start planning for and working toward an early retirement with real estate investment. It is my sincere desire that you use this book as your go-to manual for any questions you might have or the guidance you will need.

I hope that you enjoyed reading this book as much as I enjoyed writing it, and that you have learned a lot. If you found this book helpful, do leave a review for me, as I'd love to hear from you.

Cheers,

Michael Steven.

If you would like to read more, here are some other books I have written:

You can also follow me on:

My Website: https://vagpublishing.com/

Facebook: https://business.facebook.com/MichaelStevenAuthor/

Instagram: https://www.instagram.com/vagpublishing/

Twitter: https://twitter.com/publishing_v

Author Page: https://www.amazon.com/~/e/B08F814H22

# REAL ESTATE INVESTMENT CHECKLIST

## (9 Calculators That Will Help You Achieve Success!)

This checklist includes:

❏ 9 important calculators that you should use to achieve success and head towards *Financial Freedom with Real Estate*

❏ Helpful links

❏ Plus receive future updates

Forget about yesterday and start thinking about tomorrow.

*"The past and the future are separated by a second, so make that second count!" ~ Quote from Carmine Pirone*

To receive your Free Real Estate Calculators Checklist, email me at:

michael@TheBestSellerBooks.com

# REFERENCES


*(2020, January 13) "The Simple Math Behind How You Can Retire Early With Real Estate Investing." Retrieved December 2, 2020, from https://steppingstonestofi.com/retire-early-with-real-estate-investing/.*

*Abraham, Stephan A. (2020, September 26). "4 Ways to Value a Real Estate Rental Property." Retrieved December 5, 2020, from December 6, 2020, from https://www.investopedia.com/articles/mortgages-real-estate/11/how-to-value-real-estate-rental.asp.*

*Asad, Ranah. (2018, August 10). "10 Expert Tips On How To Buy Multiple Properties In Real Estate." Retrieved December 8, 2020, from https://www.mashvisor.com/blog/10-tips-how-to-buy-multiple-properties-real-estate/.*

*Brumer, Liz. (2019, December 20). "6 Ways Of Buying Rental Property With No Money Down." Retrieved December 5, 2020, from https://www.fool.com/millionacres/real-estate-investing/rental-properties/6-ways-buying-rental-property-no-money-down/#.*

*Brumer-smith, Liz. N.D. "Rental Property Investing Basics." Retrieved December 2, 2020 from https://www.fool.com/millionacres/real-estate-investing/rental-properties.*

*(2020, June 29) "Buy And Hold Real Estate Strategy: Pros, Cons, And Maximizing Your Income." Retrieved December 2, 2020, from https://sparkrental.com/buy-and-hold-real-estate-strategy/.*

*Carson, Chad. N.D. "The Free And Clear Real Estate Plan." Retrieved December 3, 2020 from https://www.coachcarson.com/the-free-clear-real-estate-plan/.*

*Carson, Chad. N.D. "How Many Rental Properties Do You Need To Retire?" Retrieved December 3, 2020 from https://www.coachcarson.com/how-many-rental-properties-to-retire/.*

*Carson, Chad. N.D. "How To Retire In 10 Years Using Real Estate Investing (3 Case Studies)." Retrieved December 3, 2020 from https://www.coachcarson.com/retire-real-estate-investing/.*

*Cockerham, Ryan. (2018, November 27). "The Average Annual Rate Of*

*Inflation For Retirement Planning." Retrieved December 2, 2020, from https://finance.zacks.com/average-annual-rate-inflation-retirement-planning-8623.html.*

*Collatz, Andrea. (2017, March 7). "How To Raise Rent Without Complaints A Straightforward Guide For Landlords On Whether To Raise Rent And Tips On How To Do It." Retrieved December 8, 2020, from https://www.mysmartmove.com/smartmove/blog/how-raise-rent-with-no-complaints.page.*

*Collins, Gord. (2019, June 2). "What Is The Best Type Of Rental Property?" Retrieved December 4, 2020, from https://managecasa.com/articles/best-type-of-rental-property/.*

*Daibes, Victoria. (2019, July 29). "7 Major Benefits Of Investing In Real Estate."Retrieved December 3, 2020, from https://www.mashvisor.com/blog/benefits-of-investing-in-real-estate/.*

*Davis, Brian. (2020, July 1). "15 Clever Ways To Come Up With A Down Payment For A Rental Property." Retrieved December 7, 2020, from https://sparkrental.com/15-clever-ways-down-payment-for-rental-property/.*

*Dogen, Sam. (2020, February 19). "'It's Hard To Frugal Your Way To Early Retirement,' Says Self-made Millionaire Who Retired At 34." Retrieved December 2, 2020, from https://www.cnbc.com/2020/02/19/hard-to-frugal-your-way-to-early-retirement-says-self-made-millionaire-who-retired-at-34.html.*

*Eberlin, Erin. (2018, September 29). "7 Times You Can Get A Property Below Market Value." Retrieved December 9, 2020, from https://www.thebalancesmb.com/types-of-distressed-properties-2124840.*

*Eberlin, Erin. (2019, February 21). "New Tenant Checklist For Landlords The Essentials To Prepare For A New Tenant."Retrieved December 8, 2020, from https://www.thebalancesmb.com/sample-landlord-checklist-for-new-tenants-2125042.*

*Eberlin, Erin. (2019, May 31). "Rental Property Is It A Good Investment?" Retrieved December 2, 2020, from https://www.thebalancesmb.com/evaluate-the-investment-property-2124820.*

*Eberlin, Erin. (2019, June 25). "How To Choose The Best Tenant For Your Rental 7 Tips For Placing A Great Tenant In Your Investment Property."*

Retrieved December 8, 2020, from https://www.thebalancesmb.com/the-right-tenant-for-your-rental-2124984.

Eberlin, Erin. (2019, July 31). "10 Issues To Address Before New Tenants Move In Prepare For A New Tenant." Retrieved December 7, 2020, from https://www.thebalancesmb.com/landlord-actions-before-move-in-2125027.

"Financing Contingency A Clause Stipulating That The Purchase Offer Is Contingent On Securing Financing." N.D. Retrieved December 7, 2020 from https://corporatefinanceinstitute.com/resources/knowledge/deals/financing-contingency/#:~:text=in%20a%20home%20sale%20and,the%20deal%20fails%20to%20close.

Fitzgerald, Ryan. (2018, December 20). "10 Next Steps After You Go Under Contract On A Home (Infographic)." Retrieved December 8, 2020, fromhttps://www.raleighrealtyhomes.com/blog/seller-accepts-your-offer-10-things-that-come-next.html.

Forty, Retire B. N.D. "How Rental Properties Can Help You Retire Early." Retrieved December 2, 2020 from https://retireby40.org/rental-properties-retire-early/.

Frankel, Matt. (2019, September 2). "Real Estate 101: How To Analyze Rental Property Investments." Retrieved December 5, 2020, from https://www.fool.com/millionacres/real-estate-investing/rental-properties/real-estate-101-how-analyze-rental-property-investments/.

Frankel, Matt. (2019, December 2). "9 Rental Property Investing Team Members You Need." Retrieved December 7, 2020, from https://www.fool.com/millionacres/real-estate-investing/articles/9-real-estate-investing-team-members-you-need/.

Frankel, Matt. (2020, May 19). "Buying An Investment Property: 3 Ways To Make Your Offer Stand Out." Retrieved December 8, 2020, from https://www.fool.com/millionacres/real-estate-investing/articles/buying-an-investment-property-3-ways-to-make-your-offer-stand-out/#.

Golhar, Abhi. (2017, September 11). "Seven Things To Consider When Buying An Investment Rental Property." Retrieved December 7, 2020, from https://www.forbes.com/sites/forbesrealestatecouncil/2017/09/11/seven-

*things-to-consider-when-buying-an-investment-rental-property/#1efa71016dad.*

*Goreham, John. (2020, March 18). "How To Evaluate A Rental Property Quickly." Retrieved December 5, 2020, from https://www.mashvisor.com/blog/how-to-evaluate-a-rental-property-quickly/.*

*Hamed, Eman. (2018, January 28). "The Exit Strategy – Key For Successful Real Estate Investing." Retrieved December 9, 2020, from https://www.mashvisor.com/blog/exit-strategy-successful-real-estate-investing/*

*Hamed, Eman. (2018, July 19). "Should Real Estate Investors Set Up An LLC For Rental Property Investments?" Retrieved December 5, 2020, from https://www.mashvisor.com/blog/set-up-llc-for-rental-property-investments/.*

*Hamed, Eman. (2019, January 5). "5 Steps To Conducting An Accurate Rental Market Analysis." Retrieved December 6, 2020, from https://www.mashvisor.com/blog/5-steps-rental-market-analysis/.*

*Hamed, Eman. (2019, September 4). "How Much To Offer On A House: An Investor's Guide." Retrieved December 8, 2020, from https://www.mashvisor.com/blog/how-much-to-offer-on-a-house/.*

*Heiner, Dustin. N.D. "14 Ways To Fund Your Rental Property Deals." Retrieved December 6, 2020, from https://www.masterpassiveincome.com/how-to-finance-your-rental-property-deal.*

*"How To Buy More Property – 10 Ways To Boost Your Portfolio." N.D. Retrieved December 5, 2020, from https://onproperty.com.au/how-to-buy-more-property/.*

*James, Gordon. (2014, October 3). "Four Simple Tips For Maintaining Your Rental Property." Retrieved December 6, 2020, from https://gordonjamesrealty.com/resource/maintaining-your-rental-property/.*

*Johnson, Holly. (2020, April 8). "Nine Things We Look For When Buying Rental Property." Retrieved December 7, 2020, from https://www.thesimpledollar.com/make-money/what-we-look-for-in-a-profitable-rental-property/.*

*Kimmons, James. (2019, November 20). "Risks To Avoid When Using Leverage In Real Estate." Retrieved December 4, 2020, from https://www.thebalancesmb.com/top-don-ts-in-using-real-estate-leverage-2867098.*

*Lake, Rebecca. (2020, February 28). "The Complete Guide To Financing An Investment Property." Retrieved December 5, 2020, from https://www.investopedia.com/articles/investing/021016/complete-guide-financing-investment-property.asp.*

*Leshnower, Ron. N.D. "When Should A Landlord Hire A Property Management Company? Hiring A Property Management Company Can Be Great For Your Business, Or Not." Retrieved December 7, 2020, from https://www.nolo.com/legal-encyclopedia/landlord-hire-property-management-company-29885.html.*

*Leusin, Timofej. (2019, October 5). "Buying Investment Property: 4 Best Tips To Get An Offer Accepted." Retrieved December 8, 2020, from https://www.mashvisor.com/blog/buying-investment-property-4-tips-offer/*

*Loudenback, Tanza. (2019, November 13). "How To Retire Early So You Can Work, Travel, And Relax On Your Own Schedule." Retrieved December 2, 2020, from https://www.businessinsider.com/personal-finance/how-to-retire-early-steps-for-early-retirement?ir=t.*

*Mccormick, Justin. N.D. "How Much Money Do I Need To Invest In Real Estate?" Retrieved December 3, 2020, from https://wealthfit.com/investing/money-needed-start-real-estate-investing/.*

*Mccormick, Justin. N.D. "Real Estate Investing: A Step-by-step Path To Early Retirement." Retrieved December 2, 2020, from https://wealthfit.com/investing/real-estate-investment-path-to-early-retirement/.*

*Moncrief, Jimmy. (2016, April 13). "5 Easy Ways To Find Quality Tenants." Retrieved December 4, 2020, from https://www.landlordology.com/top-5-ways-find-quality-tenants/.*

*Mueller, Laura. (2019, August 28). "6 Factors To Consider When Buying An Investment Property." Retrieved December 6, 2020, from https://www.moving.com/tips/6-factors-to-consider-when-buying-an-investment-property/.*

*Parker, Tim. (2017, September 17). "15 Tips For Buying Your First Rental Property." Retrieved December 5, 2020, from https://www.investopedia.com/articles/investing/090815/buying-your-first-investment-property-top-10-tips.asp.*

*Pere, David. (2020, April 6). "How To Choose The Best Real Estate Exit*

*Strategy To Avoid Failure!" Retrieved December 9, 2020, from https://www.frommilitarytomillionaire.com/best-real-estate-exit-strategy/.*

*Samurai, Financial. (2019, December 7). "How To Purchase Property Below Fair Market Value With Just A Few Words." Retrieved December 7, 2020, from https://www.financialsamurai.com/thre-ways-to-get-people-to-sell-their-property-below-fair-market-value/.*

*Scherer, David. (2017, December 12). "8 Types Of Risk Every Real Estate Investor Should Know About." Retrieved December 7, 2020, from https://origininvestments.com/2017/12/12/8-types-risk-every-real-estate-investor-know/.*

*Taylor, Mark. (2017, November 1). "How To Prepare Your Property For Rent." Retrieved December 5, 2020, from https://taylors.com.au/articles/how-to-prepare-your-property-for-rent-so-it-stands-out-from-the-crowd.*

*Teneff, Mira. (2020, April 2). "How To Calculate Rental Rate: A Beginner's Guide." Retrieved December 7, 2020, from https://www.mashvisor.com/blog/how-to-calculate-rental-rate/.*

*Unlimited, Lifestyles. N.D. "How Starting A Rental Property Business Can Retire You Faster Than Your 401k." Retrieved December 2, 2020, from https://lifestylesunlimited.com/how-starting-a-rental-property-business-can-retire-you-faster-than-401k/.*

*Vandenboss, Kevin. (2020, March 1). "What Is Leverage In Real Estate, And How Do You Use It?" Retrieved December 8, 2020, from https://www.fool.com/millionacres/real-estate-basics/real-estate-terms/what-leverage-real-estate-and-how-do-you-use-it/.*

*Weaver, Jeff. (2020, August 24). "Forming An Llc For Real Estate Investments: Pros & Cons." Retrieved December 7, 2020, from https://www.legalzoom.com/articles/forming-an-llc-for-real-estate-investments-pros-cons.*

*White, Stephen M. (2019, February 15). "How To Calculate The Rental Rate: The 5 Most Important Factors." Retrieved December 5, 2020, from https://rentprep.com/collecting-rent/how-to-calculate-rental-rate/.*

*Williams, Sean. (2019, October 24). "10 Ways To Lower Your Mortgage Rate." Retrieved December 4, 2020, from https://www.fool.com/millionacres/real-estate-financing/mortgages/10-ways-lower-your-mortgage-rate/.*

*Wolves, Financial. (2020, April 20). "15 Step Real Estate Due Diligence Checklist." Retrieved December 6, 2020, from https://financialwolves.com/real-estate-due-diligence-checklist/.*

Made in the USA
Columbia, SC
17 June 2025

59509840R00095